Great White Fleet

Celebrating
Canada Steamship Lines
Passenger Ships

BY JOHN HENRY

Foreword by the Right Honourable Paul Martin, PC, CC

DUNDURN
TORONTO

Editor: Allister Thompson
Design: Courtney Horner
Printer: Friesens

Library and Archives Canada Cataloguing in Publication

Henry, John, 1939 Dec. 11-
Great White Fleet : celebrating Canada Steamship Lines
passenger ships / John Henry.

Includes index.
Issued also in electronic formats.
ISBN 978-1-4597-1046-7

1. Canada Steamship Lines (Firm) 2. Passenger ships

--Canada--History--20th century. 3. Steamboat lines--Canada
--History--20th century. I. Title.

VM381.H45 2013   387.2'4309710904   C2012-908611-8

1   2   3   4   5   17   16   15   14   13

We acknowledge the support of the **Canada Council for the Arts** and the **Ontario Arts Council** for our publishing program. We also acknowledge the financial support of the **Government of Canada** through the **Canada Book Fund** and **Livres Canada Books**, and the **Government of Ontario** through the **Ontario Book Publishing Tax Credit** and the **Ontario Media Development Corporation**.

Printed and bound in Canada.

Visit us at
Dundurn.com
Definingcanada.ca
@dundurnpress
Facebook.com/dundurnpress

Dundurn	Gazelle Book Services Limited	Dundurn
3 Church Street, Suite 500	White Cross Mills	2250 Military Road
Toronto, Ontario, Canada	High Town, Lancaster, England	Tonawanda, NY
M5E 1M2	LA1 4XS	U.S.A. 14150

Front endpaper: When Canada Steamship Lines published this map in 1948, the company still operated steamers on the five routes that comprised the traditional core of its far-flung passenger operations. Those were, from left, Detroit-Duluth, Toronto-Queenston, Toronto-Prescott, Prescott-Montreal, and Montreal-Quebec-Chicoutimi, otherwise known as the Montreal-Saguenay service. Yellow dots indicate ports of call, including (at far right) C.S.L.'s two hotels in Quebec, the Manoir Richelieu at Murray Bay and the Hotel Tadoussac at Tadoussac. (C.S.L. brochure, author's collection.)

Rear endpaper: For years, Canada Steamship Lines proudly proclaimed itself as the "world's largest inland water transportation company," and the map, published in a corporate brochure issued near the end of World War II, illustrates what made C.S.L. so special. Shown are not only its passenger routes but also its freighter routes, hotels, grain elevators, coal docks and Davie shipbuilding subsidiary. (The flag to the left of the former Canadian flag is the old C.S.L. house flag.) (C.S.L. brochure, author's collection.)

To Sally

Contents

Foreword

This book commemorates a very different and special time in the history of transportation in Canada. It was a time when the pace of life was slower and road and air travel were not yet the chief modes of transit in our country. From 1913 to 1965, graceful Canada Steamship Lines steamers plied the waterways of the Great Lakes from Chicoutimi to Niagara and from Windsor to Duluth, taking countless passengers to their places of business or pleasure. Many Canadians will remember journeying on these ships or seeing them from afar — a symbol of the wealth of mighty waterways that make up part of this vast country that we love.

The result of John Henry's painstaking research and his love for the subject matter is his capturing the spirit of those times and its ships in a narrative and visual feast for the eyes that will not only bring back memories for those who were there but will also educate and preserve for the historical record an important part of Canada's past. Wonderfully illustrated with archival photographs, brochures, and advertisements that demonstrate the beauty of these steamships and tell their story in pictures, *The Great White Fleet* also provides the story of the company's passenger services growth, success, and eventual decline, including such events as the burning of the *Noronic* in 1949, a tragic accident that left scars on our national psyche.

But mostly this book should be viewed as a celebration of an era that will not return, of a way of travel that allowed passengers time to take in Canada's immense natural beauty at a liveable pace, especially when looking back from a fast-paced time such as the one in which we live. This book is both an important documentation and a wonderful keepsake.

When I joined C.S.L. in the early seventies the Great White Fleet was already in permanent dry dock. However, the stories of those wonderful years were still very much part of the company's lore, and heaven help the newly arrived soul who failed to acknowledge its legends. Indeed, I had a unique insight into one aspect of those stories, as Sheila in her university days before our marriage had been a waitress at the company's great hotel, the Manoir Richelieu. As a result she was forever running into friends she had met then and they would spend hours exchanging memories, most of which seemed to revolve around how disruptive it was when one of the steamships discharged its boatload of passengers at the hotel dock, requiring in turn the university-bound waitresses to do some actual work.

I have always envied Sheila's ties to C.S.L.'s past, but John Henry's research and obvious talent brings me much closer to it and I am very grateful to him for having brought a Canadian era back to life.

It is with great fondness that I invite you to take a historic literary journey on the *Richelieu* or the *Rapids Prince* through the magnificent lakes and rivers of our great land.

— The Right Honourable Paul Martin, PC, CC

Introduction

My love affair with lake and river passenger steamers began with childhood summers spent on the shores of Lake Erie. Every evening during the late 1940s you could watch an imposing paddlewheel passenger ship sail past our house on an overnight voyage from Buffalo, New York, to Detroit. By the time the company that operated the service, the venerable Detroit & Cleveland Navigation Co., ended it in 1950, I had made the trip between those cities no fewer than four times in five years. And I was hooked.

I especially cherished my grandfather's companionship on two of these voyages; his enthusiasm for them was almost as great as mine. We both loved those steamers of the D&C — there were five plying various routes on the Great Lakes when I made my first trip — for their graceful lines. With their straight stems, tall, upright stacks, particularly handsome pilothouses and just the right amount of sheer (the fore-to-aft curve of the hull), they were a delight to behold.

But there was more to arouse the senses. There was the rhythmic noise of a steamer's thrashing paddles, the sweet sight of the steady parade of passenger and cargo ships in the busy Detroit River, the crunching sound of our ship as it nudged the pilings at the D&C's ancient Third Street wharf in Detroit, and the pungent but not quite offensive smell of the heavily polluted waters by the steamer's eastern terminus in the Buffalo River. (Back then, pollution was often considered a symbol of industrial progress.)

Given these treasured experiences, it naturally followed that I would become an avid fan of an even larger fleet of passenger ships. That was the one operated by Canada Steamship Lines of Montreal on the Great Lakes and St. Lawrence River. The company's size in the mid-twentieth century has always amazed me. It's hard to overstate how awed I was as a child not yet ten years old reading this passage in a publication issued by C.S.L. late in World War II: "From a small beginning, Canada Steamship Lines now operates the largest freshwater fleet in the world, consisting of 80 ships, including passenger, package freight, upper and lower lake bulk freighters, and self-unloader freighters. The company also operates shipyards, hotels, fuel and supply services, etc."[1] A nearby multi-coloured double-page map of C.S.L.'s extensive shipping routes and shore facilities (see map inside back cover) only underscored the corporate breadth and depth.

Not surprisingly, it was the description of the company's passenger fleet that interested me most. "Marine architects point to the twelve passenger vessels of Canada

Steamship Lines as the most modern and luxurious of their type in Canadian ship-building history," the publication gushed. It went on to assert that "no inland river and lake steamers anywhere in the world are more superbly fitted out than these units in the 'great white fleet' of C.S.L."[2]

Only later did I learn that the aforementioned description took some liberties. At the time, just nine passenger vessels were in service (the other three were laid up), and to say that they were modern was a considerable stretch. Half the dozen ships were products of the Victorian or Edwardian eras. No matter. Whether still in service or inactive, whether modern or aged, these were ships an owner could be proud of — of that I am certain.

Almost all these vessels were gracefully proportioned, and some boasted the sumptuous décor in their public rooms that characterized early twentieth-century inland-water steamers. Enhancing the appearance of every C.S.L. ship was arguably one of the best colour schemes for a smoke-stack ever devised: a wonderfully subtle orange-red topped, in ascending order, by a white band and a black band.

The stack colours complemented particularly well the all-white exterior paint job sported in the 1920s and early 1930s by the company's passenger ships that operated on Lake Ontario and the St. Lawrence and Saguenay Rivers. (Thus, the "great white fleet.")

Regrettably, sometime in the 1930s C.S.L. changed the colour scheme of these ships so that they were dark green below the main deck. The change, in my opinion, deprived the vessels of some of their exterior elegance. So even though the longest surviving ships spent most of their years under the C.S.L. flag in the green and white livery, a disproportionate number of the illustrations in this book show the ships at their earlier, all-white best.

A truly comprehensive account of the company's passenger steamers would include those that once operated on Lake Ontario between Hamilton and Toronto. I omitted them because by the time these services ended in the 1920s, they weren't key components of Canada Steamship's route network. This book concentrates on the routes shown on the map titled "Your Water Playground," taken from a 1948 C.S.L. brochure. (see inside front cover.)

Growing up in Buffalo, at the eastern end of Lake Erie, and spending summers in nearby southern Ontario, I saw C.S.L passenger ships from time to time but — to my everlasting regret — never managed to sail aboard any member of the fleet. The closest I came was taking a fondly remembered trip across Lake Ontario aboard the beloved Toronto-Niagara excursion vessel *Cayuga* in 1954, when she was under different ownership.

Happily, producing this book has enabled me to learn more about what I missed. And hopefully, you too will enjoy the fruits of my research. Bon voyage!

CHAPTER 1

The Great White Fleet: An Overview

Walk into the lobby of the Canada Steamship Lines building in Montreal and the first thing you're likely to notice is a large scale model of a dazzling white passenger ship housed smartly in a glass case.

Nearly a half-century has passed since the handsome vessel that inspired the model, the *Tadoussac*, made her last voyage for the company. Canada Steamship Lines, today a part of CSL Group Inc., wound up its celebrated passenger service in 1965, and now sticks to the decidedly less glamorous (though more lucrative) business of carrying cargoes such as coal and iron ore. But it's a measure of the prominence and prestige that passenger ships like the *Tadoussac* brought the company that her replica still occupies pride of place on the ground floor of the corporate head office. As Edgar Andrew Collard observes in his history of the company, *Passage to the Sea: The Story of Canada Steamship Lines*, "Passenger ships were for Canada Steamship Lines what passenger trains were for the railways; they made the company part of people's experience, part of their lives."[2]

That helps to explain why C.S.L., virtually alone among owners of passenger steamers on North America's inland waters, planned to build new ones after World War II and why the company was among the very last to remain in the passenger business. To be sure, those ships never materialized; after their champion, the company's longtime president, W.H. Coverdale, died in 1949, its management began scaling back passenger services drastically. Even so, the *Tadoussac* and two running mates would soldier on for another sixteen years on the beautiful Montreal-Quebec City-Saguenay River route, keeping alive the romance of travel by

While the nation sleeps, the fleet moves on. Tonight, the ships of the world's greatest freshwater fleet are plowing the darkness. Deep in the ships, engines are throbbing and men are standing guard over the fires. On the bridges silent figures stand on watch. Water hisses along the ship's sides, and above, lights from the mastheads glimmer among the stars. And the passenger ships, their red, white and black funnels silhouetted in light above the glittering decks, move on their way with aloof majesty.

— from *The Saguenay Trip* by Damase Potvin[1]

Left: A scale model of the *Tadoussac* still occupies pride of place in the lobby of the Canada Steamship Lines building in Montreal. (Courtesy of the author.)

Above: A small sampling of the eighty passenger and cargo ships in the C.S.L. fleet is depicted in these illustrations from a company brochure of the mid-1940s. From left, the bulk carrier *Barrie*; the package freighter *Selkirk*; Canada's largest Great Lakes bulk carrier for more than two decades, the *Lemoyne*, and the passenger steamers *Noronic, Quebec, Cayuga, Kingston,* and *Rapids Prince*. (C.S.L. brochure, author's collection.)

Below: With their engines aft and black-and-white paint jobs, the three sister ships built for Northern Navigation Co. bore scant resemblance to C.S.L.'s passenger steamers in Eastern Canada. Here, the *Noronic*, which normally sailed Lakes Huron and Superior, enters Toronto Harbour in 1931 as the largest vessel to visit the port up to that time. (Arthur Beales photo, Toronto Port Authority PC 1/1/9447.)

steamboat that had captivated millions of Canadians and Americans.

This trio represented the last survivors of what had been a passenger fleet of breathtaking scope. Now, as C.S.L. enters its second century, it's time to recall the remarkable collection of steamers that the company operated for more than half of its existence. When it was created in 1913 from a massive consolidation of shipping companies, Canada Steamship Lines inherited some fifty vessels that were either passenger ships or passenger/freight ships.

And they could be found on the Great Lakes as far west as Duluth, Minnesota, at the head of Lake Superior, and as far east as the lower St. Lawrence River, beyond Quebec City — a distance spanning nearly 2,000 miles by C.S.L.'s calculation. This, then, was an inland water transportation company like no other.

At its outset, C.S.L., an enterprise backed by Canadian and British investors, including the powerful Furness shipping interests in London, was an amalgam of no fewer than eleven steamship companies, including seven acquired with the takeover of the formidable and long-established Richelieu and Ontario Navigation Co. (See "In the Beginning.") Some of these companies were devoted primarily to carrying passengers, others to cargo. On

Below: The *Cayuga*, one of four low-slung steamers formerly operated by the Niagara Navigation Co. on its Toronto-Niagara service, plied the same route for C.S.L. for thirty-eight years. Here, in pre-war times, the much beloved steamer clears Toronto Harbour for yet another trip across Lake Ontario to Niagara-on-the-Lake and Queenston, both in Ontario, and Lewiston, New York. (Courtesy the Jay Bascom collection.)

IN THE BEGINNING

Although Canada Steamship Lines came into being a century ago, its roots go back much farther.

They can be traced to 1845, when an enterprise in Quebec known as La Société de Navigation du Richelieu was established to carry passengers and freight between Montreal and Chambly, located ninety miles away on the Richelieu River, a tributary of the St. Lawrence River. From that humble beginning developed a shipping powerhouse that, after a merger three decades later with a vessel operator on Lake Ontario, became the Richelieu and Ontario Navigation Co. That company would gain considerably more heft in the fascinating (and complicated) lead-up to the formation of C.S.L. in 1913.

Two years earlier, the R. and O., with the backing of Britain's Furness Withy shipping company, had begun absorbing a number of inland-water steamship lines, including the Thousand Islands Steamboat Co.; the St. Lawrence River Steamboat Co.; the Niagara Navigation Co., which operated passenger service on the Toronto-Niagara and Toronto-Hamilton routes on Lake Ontario; the Northern Navigation Co., whose steamers carried passengers and package freight on Lakes Huron and Superior; and the Inland Navigation Co., which was strictly a cargo carrier.

Taken together, all these entities, plus an American subsidiary of the R. and O., formed the nucleus of something called Canada Transportation Lines Ltd., which came into being on June 19, 1913. (Before that year ended, four more companies were added and the corporate name was changed to Canada Steamship Lines Ltd.)

Today, the name Canada Steamship Lines survives in the business world but refers to the division of The CSL Group Inc. that operates approximately twenty bulk carriers on the Great Lakes-St. Lawrence Seaway system. The parent CSL Group, still headquartered in Montreal and now owned by the family of former Prime Minister Paul Martin, is a far-flung company specializing in operating self-unloading bulk-cargo ships, with operating divisions based in Australia, Asia, Europe, and the Americas.

Some of its ships, however, still sail close to home, where it all began more than 165 years ago.

the passenger side, the result of all this consolidation was as diverse and splendid an array of steamers (and steamer routes) as any ship lover could dare hope for. Let's examine the most prominent examples of what would become widely known as the Great White Fleet:

There were the distinctive engine-aft steamers built for the Northern Navigation Co., three of which C.S.L would operate for many years between Detroit and Duluth. Covering 1,600 miles on their weeklong round-trips, these elegantly appointed ships took passengers across Lakes Huron and Superior and through the incredibly busy (and fascinating) Sault Ste. Marie, or "Soo," locks on the waterway linking those lakes.

Then there were the four low-slung vessels — three of them paddle wheelers, the other propeller driven — formerly operated by the Niagara Navigation Co. for its day-excursion service across Lake Ontario between Toronto and ports on the scenic lower Niagara River. A C.S.L. booklet described the route as "one of the most popular short water trips on the continent,"[3] and that was probably no exaggeration.

Also inherited by C.S.L. were two charming Victorian-era paddle-wheel steamboats built for the Richelieu & Ontario Navigation Co., or R&O, for its overnight service on Lake Ontario that linked Toronto; Rochester, New York; and Kingston, Ontario. After leaving Kingston, the boats would pass through the enchanting Thousand Islands of the St. Lawrence River en route to Prescott, Ontario, which was as far down the river as large ships could go before the opening of the St. Lawrence Seaway in 1959. But the fun didn't stop there.

Right: The beautifully proportioned *Kingston* makes a stirring sight in pre-war days as she prepares to depart from Toronto for her overnight run across Lake Ontario to Charlotte (Rochester), New York, and then to Prescott. (Courtesy the Jay Bascom collection.)

Below: The *Rapids Prince*, the longest serving of the company's three rapids steamers, negotiates one of the most exciting parts of the route, the Long Sault Rapids, near Cornwall, Ontario. (Courtesy the Steamship Historical Society of America archives.)

Above: The *Saguenay*, built in Scotland for the Montreal-Saguenay service, arrives at Tadoussac circa 1930. (S.J. Hayward photo, Bibliothèque et Archives nationales du Québec P428.S3.SS1.D7.P44.)

Below: The *Montreal* was arguably one of the most graceful passenger steamers ever to operate for C.S.L. Along with another paddle-wheeler, the first *Quebec*, she held down the overnight service between Montreal and Quebec, first for the Richelieu and Ontario Navigation Co. and then for C.S.L. Here, the *Montreal* flaunts her good looks on her daily St. Lawrence run. (Collection Magella Bureau, Bibliothèque et Archives nationales du Québec P547.S3.SS2.D12.P5.)

Above: On display in this circa-1928 photograph at Victoria Pier in Montreal are four vessels on C.S.L.'s Montreal-Quebec and Montreal-Saguenay services. From right are the second *Quebec*, then brand-new; the *St. Lawrence*; the *Saguenay* and the *Richelieu*. (C.S.L. brochure photo, author's collection.)

Left: Passengers found that a trip on a C.S.L. steamer was a welcome antidote to the stress of city life. ("Femmes sur le pont," Madeleine Craig donation, Musée de Charlevoix.)

At Prescott, passengers would transfer to one of three rather small propeller steamers, also from the R&O company, that would make the thrilling daylight trip down the St. Lawrence to Montreal, negotiating a series of eight rapids that more risk-averse mariners bypassed by using canals. Well promoted by C.S.L. even after it reduced this service to one boat, the nine-and-a-half-hour trip included an especially treacherous set of rapids in which a steamer descended fifty-six feet in less than two miles.

Finally, there were the half dozen or so steamers employed on what would be the most famous and longest lasting C.S.L. passenger services of all: those on the Montreal-Quebec City-Saguenay route. Foremost among these vessels — all of them also from the R&O — were two impressive-looking twin-stacked paddle wheelers that operated overnight on the St. Lawrence between Montreal and Quebec City. Other vessels, including a propeller-driven British-built beauty of more recent vintage, travelled still further downriver to ports on the spectacular, fjord-like Saguenay River.

The pleasures of travelling by steamboat are nicely captured by Benny Beattie, who in his book *Tadoussac: The Sands of Summer*, describes what it was like to be a passenger aboard a C.S.L. ship making a round-trip on the Montreal-Saguenay service.

Beattie, who travelled steamers on that route from the late 1930s to the late 1950s, writes that the voyage was "a marvelous weekend vacation away from the stifling heat and noise and busyness of the city in summer," with "fresh air, water and mountains, and a couple of visits ashore — three nights of dining and dancing onboard ship, of starlit strolls along the open decks in the cool evening air as the moon danced, sparkling over the passing waters, and the dark mountainous masses towered above. Then, sleeping in clean, fresh sheets, aware of the slightest vibrations, we'd sense the ship sliding smoothly and safely through the night."[4]

With attractions like these, trips on C.S.L. vessels drew celebrities as well as ordinary folk. As Collard notes in his corporate history, no less than the Prince of Wales (later King Edward VIII) travelled aboard C.S.L. steamers on both the St. Lawrence and Lake Ontario in 1927, and the British Prime Minister Ramsay MacDonald made the Toronto-Niagara crossing a year later. Talk about a publicist's dream; this was it.

Whether celebrities or not, passengers would have travelled aboard vessels that were delights to behold, thanks to the great care that C.S.L. lavished on the exterior appearance of its steamers. It's hard to imagine a more attractive livery than the one the company had adopted for most of its passenger ships by the 1920s, which many consider to be highpoint for this side of the company's business.

This gilded, hand-carved trailboard once enhanced the port bow of the *St. Lawrence*, which operated for many years on the C.S.L.'s Montreal-Saguenay service. It hangs today in the Marine Museum of the Great Lakes at Kingston. (Ben Holthof photo, Marine Museum of the Great Lakes at Kingston.)

SAILING SCHEDULE, 1926

Subject to change without notice

TORONTO - NIAGARA RIVER

Direct connection for Niagara Falls, Buffalo and other U.S. Points.
Daylight Saving Time

A—Effective May 19th to October 10th, inclusive.
A-B—Effective May 22d to September 19th, inclusive.
A-B-C—Effective June 26th to September 12th, inclusive.

SOUTHBOUND	A	A	B	C	A	B	C
	A.M.	A.M.	A.M.	A.M.	P.M.	P.M.	P.M.
Toronto..........Lv	†7.45	§8.15	*9.15	*1130	*2.15	§4.30	†5.25	*6.30
Niagara-on-the-Lake.Lv	9.45	10.15	11.25	1.40	4.15	6.35	7.30	8.30
Queenston........Ar	10.25	10.45	12.00	2.30	4.45	7.10	8.20	9.15
Lewiston..........Ar	10.15	11.00	12.10	2.10	5.00	7.20	8.05	9.00
	A.M.	A.M.	A.M.	P.M.	P.M.	P.M.	P.M.	P.M.

NORTHBOUND	C	A	A	B	C	A	B	C
	A.M.	A.M.	A.M.	P.M.	P.M.	P.M.	P.M.	P.M.
Lewiston..........Lv	*8.40	†1015	§1110	*1.10	*3.15	*6.35	*8.15	§9.05
Queenston.........Lv	8.25	10.30	10.50	12.00	2.50	5.50	8.30	9.15
Niagara-on-the-Lake.Lv	9.05	11.00	11.35	1.35	3.40	7.00	9.00	9.40
Toronto..........Ar	11.15	1.00	1.45	◆3.45	5.50	9.00	11.10	11.45
	A.M.	P.M.	P.M.	P.M.	P.M.	P.M.	P.M.	P.M.

At Lewiston, N. Y., all steamers connect with Niagara Gorge cars which meet New York Central trains at Niagara Falls Station, for and from Buffalo and other United States points. Direct connection at Queenston, Ont., with the International Railway Co. for and from Niagara Falls and Buffalo.

◆ Connecting with steamer leaving Toronto 4.00 p.m. for Rochester, Thousand Islands, Montreal, etc. † Daily except Sunday. * Daily. § Sunday only.

TORONTO - ROCHESTER - MONTREAL

EASTBOUND READ DOWN		Effective May 25th to June 12th and September 13th to 25th Tues., Thur. and Sat. June 14th to Sept. 11th, Daily	WESTBOUND READ UP	
Eastern Standard Time	Daylight Saving Time		Daylight Saving Time	Eastern Standard Time
P.M.	P.M.		A.M.	A.M.
* 3.00	4.00	Lv Toronto (Yonge St. Wharf) Ar	7.00	6.00
9.15	10.15	Ar.‡Rochester (Municipal) Lv	12.00	11.00
9.45	10.45	Lv..Rochester) Docks (..Ar	11.30	10.30
* 4.45	5.45	Ar...Kingston (Swift's)..Lv	5.20	4.20
5.00	6.00	Lv.▲ Kingston (Wharf)..Ar	5.10	4.10
6.35	7.35	Lv.*Clayton (N.Y. C. Dock)..Lv	3.50	2.50
7.15	8.15	Lv...Alexandria Bay...Lv	3.10	2.10
* 8.30	9.30	Lv...Brockville §.....Lv	1.50	12.50
* 9.20	10.20	Ar...Prescott (C. P. R.)..Lv	12.50	11.50
9.30	10.30	Lv...Prescott) Dock (..Ar	8.00	7.00
12.30	1.30	Lv...Cornwall.....Lv	12.00	11.00
5.45	6.45	Ar....Montreal......Lv	1.00	12.00
P.M.	P.M.		A.M.	NOON

*Daylight Saving Time in effect locally. ● Connection with New York Central Railway special sleeping cars from New York City, Buffalo and western points; commencing June 28th connection with New York Central through sleeping car leaving Chicago 8.25 a.m. (standard time), Cleveland 6.00 p.m., direct to steamer's wharf at Clayton. ‡ Street cars from all parts of the city of Rochester connect with street cars leaving corner of St. Paul and Main Streets every forty minutes for Rochester Municipal Docks. § Connecting with Canadian National International Limited Train, westbound, leaving Montreal 10.00 a.m. Standard Time; 11.00 a.m. Daylight Saving Time, also Canadian Pacific train leaving Ottawa 9.20 a.m. Standard Time; 10.20 a.m. Daylight Saving Time.

▲ Connection with Canadian National Railways special sleeping cars leaving Toronto 11.00 p.m. standard time (12.00 M'T. daylight saving time).

TORONTO - THOUSAND ISLANDS - BAY OF QUINTE

Eastbound via American Channel Thousand Islands Route READ DOWN		STEAMER "CAPE TRINITY" Effective Eastbound July 17th to August 28th Mon., Thur. and Sat. Effective Westbound July 18th to August 29th Tue., Fri. and Sun.	Westbound via Canadian Channel, the Scenic Bay of Quinte Route READ UP	
Eastern Standard Time	Daylight Saving Time		Daylight Saving Time	Eastern Standard Time
P.M.	P.M.		A.M.	A.M.
3.00	4.00	Lv.....Toronto.....Ar	8.30	7.30
5.45	6.45	Lv...Alexandria Bay....	....	....
....	....	.......Belleville....Lv	9.00	8.00
....	....	.......Kingston....Lv	3.00	2.00
....	....	.......Kingston....Ar	2.45	1.45
8.00	9.00	Ar....Prescott.....Lv	9.45	8.45
A.M.	A.M.		A.M.	A M.

A.M. Light Type; P.M. Heavy Type.

1

MONTREAL - QUEBEC
Season—May to November

EASTBOUND READ DOWN		Until May 22d and after September 26th daily except Sunday May 23d to Sept. 26th daily. Dates inclusive	WESTBOUND READ UP	
Eastern Standard Time	Daylight Saving Time		Daylight Saving Time	Eastern Standard Time
P.M.	P.M.		A.M.	A.M.
6.30	7.30	Lv.....Montreal....Ar	7.00	6.00
9.15	10.15	Lv.....Sorel......Lv	2.30	1.30
12.15	1.15	Lv...Three Rivers...Lv	11.30	10.30
6.00	7.00	Ar......Quebec....Lv	6.00	5.00
A.M.	A.M.		P.M.	P.M.

MONTREAL AND QUEBEC - MURRAY BAY - TADOUSAC - SAGUENAY RIVER

EASTBOUND—READ DOWN		Spring and Autumn Schedule Daylight Saving Time	WESTBOUND — READ UP	
S.S. Cape Diamond May 14 to July 6 and Sept. 9 to Oct. 24 Tues. & Fri.	S.S. Saguenay June 15 to July 2 and Sept. 7 to 24 Tues. & Fri.		S.S. Cape Diamond May 16 to July 8 and Sept. 9 to Oct. 24 Thur. & Sun.	S.S. Saguenay June 18 to July 5 and Sept. 10 to 27 Fri. & Mon.
A.M.	P.M.		A.M.	A.M.
....	7.35	Lv.....Montreal.....Ar	....	9.30
....	5.00	Ar.....Quebec......Lv	....	9.00
8.00	7.00	Lv.....Quebec......Ar	6.00	[8.45
12.15	....	Lv...Eboulements...Lv	10.30	....
1.30	12.00	Lv...St. Irenee...Lv	9.30	3.40
2.00	12.30	Ar...Murray Bay...Lv	9.00	3.20
2.20	1.00	Lv...Murray Bay...Lv	7.00	2.30
2.50	1.30	Lv...Cap a l'Aigle...Lv	6.20	2.00
4.30	2.45	Lv...St. Simeon...Lv	4.45	1.00
7.00	4.45	Ar....Tadousac....Lv	2.30	11.15
According	5.30	Lv...L'Anse St. Jean...Ar	According	10.45
to	10.30	Ar.....Bagotville....Lv (St. Alphonse)	to	7.00
tide		Ar...Chicoutimi....Lv	tide	
Wed. & Sat. A.M.	Wed. & Sat. P.M.		Wed. & Sat. A.M.	Thur. & Sun. A.M.

MONTREAL AND QUEBEC - MURRAY BAY - TADOUSAC - SAGUENAY RIVER

EASTBOUND—READ DOWN			Summer Schedule Daylight Saving Time Effective July 6 to Sept. 4	WESTBOUND—READ UP		
S.S. Cape Diamond Mon. Thur. & Sat.	S.S. Saguenay Mon. & Thur.	S.S. Richelieu Tues.	S.S. Richelieu Fri.	S.S. Cape Diamond Tues. Fri. & Sun.	S.S. Saguenay Thur. & Sun.	S.S. Richelieu Fri.	S.S. Richelieu Mon.
A.M.	P.M.	P.M.	P.M.		P.M.	A.M.	A.M.	A.M.
.....	7.35	7.35	7.35	Lv.....Montreal....Ar	.....	9.30	9.30	9.30
.....	5.00	5.00	5.00	Ar.....Quebec....Lv	.....	9.00	9.00	9.00
8.00	7.00	7.00	6.00	Lv.....Quebec....Ar	10.30	8.45	8.45	8.45
12.15				Lv Eboulements Lv	6.00			
1.30				Lv...St. Irenee...Lv	5.00			
2.00	12.00	11.30	10.00	Ar..Murray Bay...Lv	4.30	4.15	4.30	4.30
2.20	12.30	1.00	11.45	Lv..Murray Bay...Lv	4.00	2.45	2.30	2.00
.....				Lv..Cap a l'Aigle..Lv				
4.30				Lv...St. Simeon...Lv	2.15			
7.00	4.00	4.00	2.45	Ar....Tadousac...Lv	12.00	11.15	11.30	11.00
According	6.30	6.30	3.00	Lv...Tadousac....Ar	According	11.00	11.15	6.00
to				Lv L'Anse St. Jean Ar	to			
tide	10.30	10.30	7.00	Ar.⊙Bagotville ⊙.Lv (St. Alphonse)	tide	7.00	7.15	2.15
Tues. Fri. &Sun.	Tues. & Fri.	Wed.	Sat.	Ar..Chicoutimi..Lv	Tues. Fri. & Sun.	Wed. & Sat.	Thur.	Sun.
A.M.	P.M.	P.M.	P.M.		A.M.	A.M.	A.M.	A.M.

Note—For S.S. Cape Eternity weekly cruise, see pages 3 and 4.
⊙ No call Bagotville.　　A.M. Light Type; P.M. Heavy Type.

IMPORTANT NOTICE

Time tables show the time steamers should arrive at and leave different ports, but their departure, arrival or connection at time stated is not guaranteed, nor does the Company hold itself responsible for any delay or any consequences arising therefrom. All times subject to fluctuation from stress of weather, etc., and change with or without notice. If call cannot be made with safety, Company reserves the right to cancel stop at any port.

2

This timetable illustrates the close connections between steamers on the various "Niagara to the Sea" routes. (Author's collection.)

Depicted on the cover of C.S.L.'s brochure for 1926 are the lovely *Saguenay*, at right, and the *Cape Eternity* as they meet in the spectacular Saguenay River. Watching over them from Cape Trinity is the Virgin Mary — or, rather, a statue of her that was one of the most memorable sights on the voyage. (Author's collection.)

CANADA'S FINEST CRUISE »
« NIAGARA-TO-THE-SEA

SCENIC THRILLS!
HISTORIC BACKGROUND!
OLD WORLD CITIES!
SAGUENAY RIVER!
NEW FRANCE!

A thousand-mile fresh-water trip through the land of the voyageurs. Every mile redolent with the spirit of romance and adventure, bringing to life again the early French explorers, the swash-buckling soldiery, the cowled priesthood, the Indians, Cartier, Wolfe, Champlain, Montcalm, the "Plains of Abraham"—New France!

See America's greatest cataract — Niagara — the enchanting Thousand Islands, shoot the roaring Rapids of the St. Lawrence, view the sublime spectacle of Saguenay's capes — Trinity and Eternity — see modern Toronto, cosmopolitan Montreal and ancient Quebec — first outposts of the continent's civilization . . . And see it all from the wide-spreading decks of a luxurious Canada Steamship Lines' steamer — go aboard at Lewiston, Queenston, Toronto, Rochester, Clayton, Alexandria Bay, Prescott, Montreal or Quebec — and enjoy a real holiday for a week or a day!

And fill full your cup of joy by enjoying en route the hospitality of the splendid Tadoussac and Manoir Richelieu hotels at Tadoussac and Murray Bay — two of America's most delightful resorts!

Text in yellow inside the 1931 brochure succinctly captures the charms of various attractions along the "Niagara to the Sea" route. The Quebec City skyline, bottom, plays a supporting role. (Author's collection.)

Right: The *Saguenay* passes the base of Cape Trinity. (C.S.L. photo, Marine Museum of the Great Lakes at Kingston.)

Below: Undated ad. (Author's collection.)

Passing Cape Trinity

Higher than Gibraltar

Passing Capes "Trinity" and "Eternity" on the route of

Niagara to the Sea

THE most satisfying trip in America for health and recreation. Almost 1000 miles of lakes, rivers and rapids, including the Thousand Islands, the exciting descent of the marvelous rapids, the historic associations of Montreal, Quaint old Quebec with its famous miracle-working shrine of Ste. Anne de Beaupré and the renowned Saguenay River with its stupendous Capes, "Trinity" and "Eternity," higher than Gibraltar.

Send 2c postage for illustrated booklet, map and guide, to John F. Pierce, Assistant Passenger Traffic Manager, Canada Steamship Lines, 129 R. & O. Bl'dg, Montreal, Canada.

CANADA STEAMSHIP LINES

Smokestacks on all the ships were repainted in the ever-so-handsome red, white, and black scheme that the old Northern Navigation Co. had favoured for its steamers on the upper Great Lakes. (In an inspired touch, the stacks were illuminated at night.)

And while the Northern Navigation ships kept their rather sombre livery of black hulls and white upper works, C.S.L. soon gave all its other passenger steamers an elegant all-white paint job that conferred on them a regal appearance. Most of the company's steamers on the St. Lawrence and Lake Ontario were further enhanced by gold-coloured trailboards — elaborate hand-carved wooden ornamentation on each side of their bows. (The trailboards, like the all-white paint scheme, disappeared before World War II, both being perhaps too costly to maintain.)

Fortunately, even as other operators of inland-water passenger boats were scaling back their routes or quitting the business altogether, C.S.L. kept the route network it acquired largely intact for more than thirty-five years. The result was a superb interconnected system enabling a passenger

C.S.L.'s passenger steamers brought business to the company's hotels like the Manoir Richelieu at Murray Bay (LaMalbaie), shown here. (Author's collection.)

to disembark from one company steamer and walk across the pier to board another that was waiting to depart within minutes on a different route.

It was a system unmatched on North America's inland waters, and it meant one could sail all the way from the Niagara River to the Saguenay River — a distance of nearly 700 miles — on four different C.S.L. ships in three days. "Niagara to the Sea" was the company's famous slogan for the entire trip. (This was an exaggeration since the lower St. Lawrence and the Saguenay, while containing saltwater, weren't actually "the Sea." But it was exaggeration in the service of promoting what was, by all accounts, a deeply satisfying voyage.)

While C.S.L. did largely preserve the routes of its predecessor companies for many years, the number of ships it operated on them shrank fairly steadily. From its peak strength of fifty-one passenger and passenger/freight boats at Canada

Steamship's inception in 1913, the fleet had shrunk to thirty-one passenger steamers by 1921 and to nineteen a decade later. By the start of the 1949 season, the last year that the company operated ships on all of its traditional routes, the passenger fleet was down to just nine ships, including one in long-term lay-up.

The Great Depression, fires and accidents, and growing competition from highway and air travel had all taken their toll — more about which later in this and subsequent chapters.

Nonetheless, the company actually added four fine propeller steamers to the Montreal-Quebec-Saguenay route in the 1920s. While other steamboat operators also were expanding their fleets at the same time in what turned out to be a final burst of corporate confidence in the future of steamboat travel, C.S.L. was better positioned than most to recoup its investment in its new vessels.

For one thing, the route down the St. Lawrence from Montreal was exceptionally scenic and represented a yet-to-be-fully-exploited market for cruises and package tours. Not only did this route include historic Quebec City, but it also offered the breathtaking splendours of the Saguenay River, where steamers sailed beneath two capes, each of them nearly 2,000 feet high — "Higher than Gibraltar," boasted C.S.L. — rising from water hundreds of feet deep.

That the rugged north shore of the St. Lawrence east of Quebec City didn't easily lend itself to road building protected, at least for a time, the Saguenay service from the automotive competition that was undoubtedly eroding business on some other C.S.L. routes in the 1920s, and causing problems for steamboat operators almost everywhere.

There was another advantage to improving the Montreal-Saguenay service: it transported passengers directly to the two beautifully situated summer hotels along the St. Lawrence in Quebec that C.S.L. had acquired with its takeover of the Richelieu & Ontario. Those were the Manoir Richelieu at Murray Bay (La Malbaie) and the Hotel Tadoussac, in the village of the same name, where the Saguenay flows into the St. Lawrence. Upgrading passenger service on the route made perfect sense since the relationship between the steamers and the hotels was mutually beneficial; each generated business for the other.

As befits a company once described as "one of Canada's largest industrial empires,"[5] C.S.L. possessed an additional advantage that other steamboat operators lacked: its own shipyard. So it was to the company's

Davie Shipbuilding & Repairing subsidiary in Lauzon, Quebec, across the St. Lawrence from Quebec City, that the company turned when reconditioning an American-built steamer that became the highly successful deluxe cruise ship *Richelieu*. Several years later, the yard launched the passenger boat *St. Lawrence* and then two slightly larger versions, the *Tadoussac* and the *Quebec*, nearly identical sister ships.

This trio of new-builds for the Montreal-Saguenay service represented the only passenger ships that were completed for C.S.L. itself; all the others in its fleet had been constructed for its corporate predecessors. At various times, however, the company also contemplated ordering new ships for its Detroit-Duluth, Toronto-Niagara and Toronto-Prescott services only to change its mind. To read C.S.L.

documents is to learn about what might have been and never was, and they are tantalizing, indeed.

Thus, a C.S.L. in-house publication reported in early 1930, even as the Depression was gathering momentum, that plans were completed for new passenger steamers that would be built when the level of patronage justified such a step. And when World War II was raging and gas rationing was prompting travellers to forsake cars for ships, it looked as if some new steamers might actually be added for the first time in two decades.

"Everybody is anxious to know the company's plans with respect to postwar conditions," Coverdale, C.S.L.'s president, told shareholders in 1944. Coverdale, who led the company from 1922 to 1949, went on to identify "what might be called certain

The *Tadoussac*, nearly identical to the *Quebec*, also was completed for C.S.L. by Davie in 1928. (Courtesy The Steamship Historical Society of America archives.)

weak spots in the fleet — one of which is the passenger service on Lake Ontario. The first improvement the company has committed itself to undertake, as soon as the facilities are obtainable and as soon as the war restrictions are lifted, will be a new passenger steamer for Lake Ontario at an estimated cost of $2 million."[6] He wasn't finished.

"The second item, which will closely follow the first," he continued, "will be a new passenger ship on the Northern Navigation Division" for the Detroit-Duluth route, "where one of the ships must be replaced at the earliest possible time."[7]

Later in 1944, Coverdale added a third hotel on the St. Lawrence to C.S.L.'s line-up, the fifty-room Thousand Islands Club on Wellesley Island, opposite Alexandria Bay, New York, a longtime company port of call. He assured the company's directors that the acquisition was expected to bring additional revenue to the Toronto-Prescott service, especially since the company was contemplating the construction of a new ship for Lake Ontario. (The ship would cross the lake before sailing through the Thousand Islands to Prescott.)

Viewed one way, Coverdale's optimism about the future of C.S.L.'s passenger steamers seems justified.

Although this side of the business had accounted for more than forty percent of corporate revenues in the mid-1920s, it still represented a significant share two decades later. In 1946, revenues from passengers accounted for twenty-six percent of the total, up three percentage points from the previous year. Coverdale's rosy prediction to C.S.L. shareholders in early 1945 that "there is plenty of business in sight, both passenger and freight"[8] was holding up.

Viewed from the perspective of overall corporate strategy, however, his priorities seem askew. When he made that rosy prediction in 1945, C.S.L. was a company operating fifty-nine freight vessels and just nine passenger vessels. It was freight, not passengers, that was driving Canada Steamship's fortunes; yet it planned to order as many new passenger ships as freighters.

In fact, within months after Coverdale's death at age 78 in August 1949, the company's priorities would change dramatically. In October, his successor as president, Col. K.R. Marshall, told C.S.L.'s executive committee that consideration should be given to selling the money-losing Thousand Islands Club, a pet project of Coverdale's. (The company soon ended its involvement in the club.) And in December, C.S.L. decided to discontinue the company's money-losing overnight passenger service between Toronto and Prescott and the rapids service between Prescott and Montreal, thereby eliminating in a single stroke two of the four links in the C.S.L.'s vaunted "Niagara-to-the-Sea" route network.

This decision naturally had the additional consequence of killing the company's aforementioned plans to build a replacement for its aging *Kingston* on the Toronto-Prescott run.

What had doomed the *Kingston* was not only her disappointing financial performance but the distinct possibility that the company would have to invest more money in the 48-year-old boat to bring her into compliance with the tighter safety regulations anticipated as a result of the tragic end in September 1949 of C.S.L.'s last remaining passenger steamer on the Detroit-Duluth run, the *Noronic*. A fire aboard the ship while she was docked in Toronto took the

W.H. Coverdale, C.S.L.'s leading advocate for passenger steamers during his 27 years as president, wore several hats. At the same time as he headed Canada's biggest shipping company, Coverdale, whose primary residence was in New York City, served as president and chairman of a major U.S. steamship operator, American Export Lines, and held the same posts at a prominent U.S. railroad, Seaboard Railway. But Coverdale, who was born in Kingston, never lost interest in the culture of his native country and assembled a renowned collection of Canadian historical art, some of which may be found in the National Gallery of Canada. (C.S.L. brochure photo, author's collection.)

lives of 118 passengers. (Not surprisingly, nothing was ever heard again from C.S.L. about plans for a new steamer on the *Noronic's* route.)

The company began the 1950 season with five passenger vessels — the quartet of Montreal-Saguenay boats added to the fleet in the 1920s and one on the Toronto-Niagara service — but ended the year with just four. Less than a year after fire destroyed the *Noronic*, it claimed the *Quebec* as she was steaming down the St. Lawrence toward Tadoussac. This time, all but seven of the ship's 426 passengers survived.

Nineteen fifty-one brought still more retrenchment. The remaining Niagara boat,

C.S.L.'s beloved *Cayuga*, was retired at the end of the season and put up for sale after several years of large operating losses. In fact, the company's entire passenger and hotel operation ran in the red that year, prompting Canada Steamship's dynamic new president, T.R. McLagan, to assert that if the losses continued, C.S.L. would have to consider abandoning both businesses.

Results actually got better in the next two years, with McLagan informing shareholders of a "substantial improvement"[9] in passenger earnings in 1952 and further improvement in 1953. Over the next decade, there are few mentions of the passenger service in the minutes of C.S.L. board meetings, although there are fleeting references to unspecified profit declines on that side of the business in 1960 and 1961. And by 1964 McLagan was speaking of the likely discontinuance of passenger operations in the next few years.

The fateful day for the Great White Fleet actually arrived quite quickly. On Tuesday, October 5, 1965, the board of Canada Steamship Lines voted to authorize the company's management to discontinue all operations of passenger ships and to sell them for scrap. C.S.L. broke the news to the public a few weeks later with a terse, 150-word statement that, alluding to new federal government safety regulations, said "the cost of altering or replacing these vessels to conform with modern standards is both prohibitive and impractical." The statement went on to say, "The inroads of automobile and air traffic have gradually reduced the use of these ships by the public to the point where economic operation is no longer possible."[10]

It was left to others to pay tribute to a steamship service that had pleasured people for generations but would no more. Montreal's *Gazette* newspaper rose to the occasion. Referring to C.S.L.'s last three passenger steamers, the paper's editorial page said:

"To see these ships sailing down the St. Lawrence in the dark, changing course from one lighted buoy to another, or to be up early in the morning to see the approach of the huge cliff of Quebec from the water, or to sense the freshening air of the lower St. Lawrence and the solemnity of the fjord of the Saguenay — these are memories worth having."[11]

Who would disagree?

CHAPTER 2

The "Niagara" in "Niagara to the Sea"

As Canada Steamship Lines envisioned it, the first leg of the ideal trip from "Niagara to the Sea" began where none of its steamers would dare venture.

That place was Niagara Falls itself, where the water from the four upper Great Lakes tumbles 160 feet to a gorge below. While the falls were — needless to say — off-limits to the company's lake and river vessels, C.S.L. encouraged customers to start their journey with a visit to the cataract it called "one of the greatest and most awe-inspiring scenic wonders of North America."[1] Presumably exhilarated by the majesty of the falls, the soon-to-be ship passengers would then board an electric interurban train (or, in later years, a bus) and travel a dozen or so miles to a dock below the falls, on the lower Niagara River. There, one of the company's handsome excursion steamers to Toronto would await them. They were in for a treat.

Once the steamer cast off, she would spend approximately a half hour sailing down the Niagara River on what C.S.L. described as "one of the most picturesque little daylight cruises in Canada."[2] This was not public relations hype, as I can attest from a fondly remembered voyage in the 1950s.

In this part of the trip, the ship, as a company booklet noted, would pass "rolling shores of vivid green" and "high cliff edges along the river bank" where "the stately homes of Canada look down."[3] As the steamer neared the mouth of the river, she would stop briefly to take on passengers at Niagara-on-the-Lake, Ontario, a one-time capital of the long-ago British province of Upper Canada turned fashionable summer resort for residents of Toronto and Buffalo, New York. Now, though, it was time for a change in scenery.

Leaving Niagara-on-the-Lake, the steamer would begin a voyage of two hours or so across the western end of Lake Ontario to Toronto. When the shoreline had receded and the broad expanse of the lake lay ahead, it was a good time to explore the ship and sample her pleasures, which were elaborate by today's standards for day-excursion vessels.

A 1931 C.S.L. brochure tells us, for instance, that the two boats then operating the Niagara-Toronto service, the *Cayuga* and the *Chippewa*, were equipped not only with a "fountain buffet" but also a dining room (mahogany-panelled in the Cayuga's case) and not just a general saloon, or lounge, where all passengers could relax, but also a genteel "ladies' cabin."[4]

The *Cayuga*, the longest serving of the four steamers that once operated for C.S.L. on the route, was particularly thoughtfully designed. Describing the ship before her completion, the magazine *Railway and Marine World* said that her general saloon, extending the full width of the vessel, was fitted with a series of bay

An artist's depiction of the *Cayuga* graces this perky C.S.L. brochure cover from the 1920s; the other steamers alluded to are the *Chippewa* and *Corona*. (Hoopes Donation, Musée de Charlevoix.)

windows "so that views may be had ahead and astern as well as straight out."[5]

Each of the bays created with this design would contain seats so small parties could keep together, the magazine reported, and two of the bays — one on each side — would be finished as private parlours for passengers who desired to be left alone.

That the steamers on the Niagara service were so well designed is not surprising. The paddle-wheeler *Chippewa* of 1893 came from the drawing board of the most famous Great Lakes naval architect of all, Frank E. Kirby, the man responsible for the magnificent (and massive) twentieth-century paddlers built for the Lake Erie overnight services of the Cleveland & Buffalo Transit Co. and the Detroit & Cleveland Navigation Co. The propeller-driven *Cayuga* of 1906 and the somewhat smaller *Corona* of 1896, another paddler, were the handiwork of Arendt Angstrom, considered by some to be second only to Kirby for the beauty of his vessels.

What these three ships on the Niagara route had in common were two nicely raked stacks, a graceful sheer (fore-to-aft curve to their hulls) and long, open decks forward of their pilothouses. The pilothouses themselves

Cayuga's ornate general saloon (lounge), featured bay windows, like those at right, to give passengers views forward and astern as well as straight ahead. (Courtesy the Jay Bascom collection.)

Above: *Corona* was another fine design of Arendt Angstrom's. (It was customary for paddle-wheelers to display their name over the paddle-wheel enclosures.) (Courtesy the Jay Bascom collection.)

Below: The *Chippewa*, shown in the Niagara River, wasn't the handsomest of the Great Lakes paddle-wheelers that the illustrious Frank E. Kirby designed, but photographed from certain angles she still could make an impressive sight. (Courtesy the Jay Bascom collection.)

Right: The *Cayuga*, seen in the Niagara River approaching Queenston in 1923, could be exhibit A for the enormous talent of her naval architect, Arendt Angstrom. (M.O. Hammond photo, S.S. Cayuga in river, Queenston, F1075-13, Archives of Ontario.)

Below: Seen from astern, the *Chippewa*, pictured in the Niagara River, could look ungainly. Note the walking beam between the stacks, so named because of its rocking action when the ship is under way. Fenders dragging the water protected the steamer when docking. (Courtesy The Steamship Historical Society of America archives.)

were triumphs in design and finish. The Toronto marine historian Jay Bascom has written that he considers the *Chippewa's* wheelhouse, with its beautiful blue name-board with gold lettering curving around its front, to be among Kirby's best. And he applauds Angstrom's pilothouse for the *Cayuga* for "its tall sectioned windows, its flying-bridge wings, its open bridge," as well as for its tasteful wood and canvas nameboard.[6] Overall, though, the *Chippewa* was considered to be the least comely; her extraordinarily broad beam and walking beam engine gave her an awkward appearance for which even her fine wheelhouse couldn't fully compensate.

The steamers looked their loveliest, in my opinion, in the 1920s, after their stacks received C.S.L.'s signature red, white, and black colours and their black hulls were painted white to match their superstructures. (In the early 1930s, the hulls of the *Chippewa* and *Cayuga* were repainted dark green and the colour of their boot topping at the waterline was changed from red to orange; their superstructures remained white.)

The fourth Niagara steamer, the *Chicora,* had the most remarkable career of all.

Built in England in 1864 as a blockade runner for the Confederacy during the Civil War, the *Chicora* served after the conflict as an overnight steamer on the upper lakes, a troop carrier, and as a yacht for the Canadian governor general before inaugurating service on the Niagara-Toronto run for the newly established Niagara Navigation Co. in 1878. (That company, which would go on to add the aforementioned *Chippewa, Corona,* and *Cayuga,* was acquired by Richelieu and Ontario Navigation just before it became part of Canada Steamship Lines.)

Even though she predated her sisters by many years, the *Chicora* underwent a modernization in 1904 that gave her a rough resemblance to the attractive *Chippewa* and *Corona.* Once the *Cayuga* entered service,

Postcard shows, from left, *Chippewa, Cayuga,* and *Corona* before they adopted C.S.L.'s colour scheme of the 1920s. (Author's collection.)

Three of the Canada Steamship Company's Fleet.

however, the *Chicora* became a spare boat and lasted on the Niagara route only through 1913, the year C.S.L. took over; the company retired her from passenger service altogether at the end of the next season, a full fifty years after her launching.

Despite the *Chicora's* retirement, C.S.L. was able to offer an impressive frequency of sailings on the route. The schedule for 1926, for example, reveals that the company was able to offer six round-trips daily on the Niagara-Toronto service during the peak of the summer travel season. If they ran full, the three remaining ships could move people in large numbers: the *Corona* was licensed to carry 1,450 passengers and the *Chippewa* and *Cayuga* each as many as 2,150 (although the *Cayuga's* capacity was reduced to 1,850 after World War II because of safety concerns).

For many years, a steamer would begin and end her trips on the lower Niagara River at two ports across from each other, one on the American side, at Lewiston, New York, and the other on the Canadian side, at Queenston, Ontario. For decades, travellers coming from Niagara Falls could reach the dock at Lewiston by the scenic electric interurban line of the Niagara Gorge Railway. Similarly, on the Cana-

The former Confederacy blockade runner *Chicora* is shown in Niagara Navigation Co. colours before she was modernized. (Courtesy the Jay Bascom collection.)

dian side, travellers coming from the Falls to the wharf at Queenston could get there on the electric interurban cars operated by the International Railway Co. It took a steamer ten to fifteen minutes to get from one terminal to the other and pick up passengers there; then she would head downriver on the charming voyage to Niagara-on-the-Lake.

Carrying passengers was big business when this impressive line-up of steamers on the Toronto waterfront in 1918 was photographed before the season began. Included among them are the *Chippewa* (foreground); the *Toronto*, used on C.S.L.'s Toronto-Prescott service, behind her; and the *Corona* to the left of and behind the *Toronto*. In the background are the two closely spaced stacks of the *Toronto's* running mate, the *Kingston*, and, to the right of her, the bow of the *Cayuga*, pointed toward the harbour. Not until the early 1920s would C.S.L. adopt an all-white livery for these ships. (Courtesy The Steamship Historical Society of America archives.)

Schedules were set so that one ship a day from Lewiston/Queenston would arrive in Toronto in time for passengers to transfer to C.S.L.'s overnight steamer to Rochester, New York, the Thousand Islands, and Prescott, Ontario. Such passengers presumably had to move briskly at the Toronto terminal since the latter boat departed just fifteen minutes after the steamer from Niagara arrived.

Business was brisk enough on the Niagara route in the late teens and early 1920s that C.S.L. asked Angstrom to prepare plans for a new and, apparently much larger, steamer for the service. She would be able to carry up to 4,000 passengers — nearly double the capacity

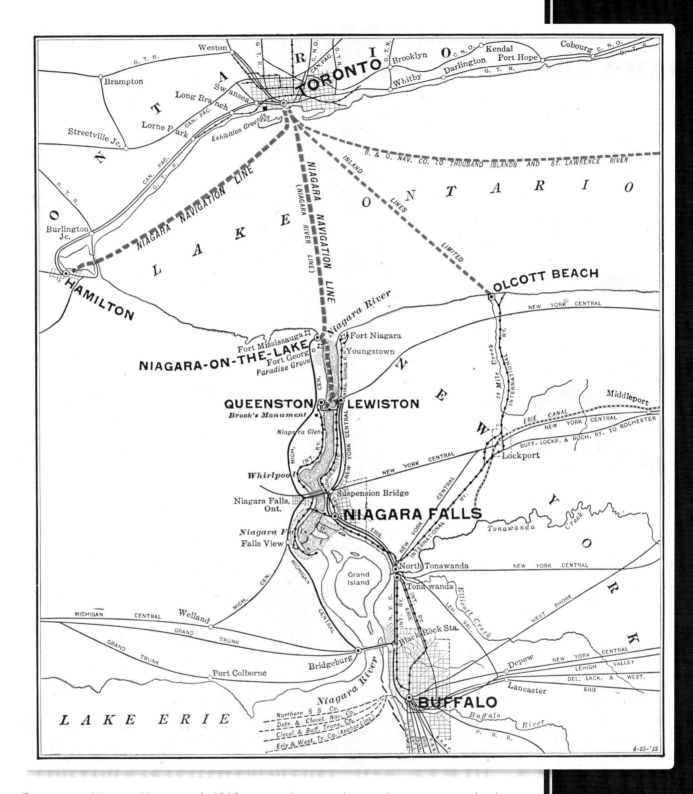

This map for Niagara Navigation's 1913 season illustrates the excellent steamer and rail connections for the Toronto-Niagara service. Shortly before its ships entered the C.S.L. fleet, the company had taken over passenger service between Toronto and Hamilton. (Author's collection.)

Left: Here's how the Lewiston, New York, terminal looked after a major makeover in 1926. (C.S.L. photo, Marine Museum of the Great Lakes at Kingston.)

Below: C.S.L.'s Toronto spacious passenger terminal, located between Bay and Yonge Streets, is shown in May 1928, less than a year after its completion. From left are the *Toronto*, *Corona*, *Cayuga*, and *Kingston*. (Arthur Beales photo, Toronto Port Authority PC 1/1/7842.)

of the *Chippewa* and the *Cayuga* in that era — and offer such amenities as a children's playground and movies. According to the minutes of a 1920 board meeting, C.S.L. directors were reminded by the company's president, Joseph Norcross, that the Niagara-Toronto line was one of best-paying in the fleet and that it was necessary to protect the company's interests by providing the best possible service on the route.

The proposed vessel was never built and board-meeting minutes of the period don't reveal the reason. But they do show that in 1923, three years after Norcross made his pitch for the new ship, the Niagara service made the smallest contribution to C.S.L.'s profits of any of the company's passenger divisions. The minutes don't indicate whether that was an aberration or part of a long-term trend.

If the Niagara fleet didn't receive the modernization once proposed for it, two important shore installations on the route did. In 1926, the terminal at Lewiston was rebuilt, and the following year the Prince of Wales opened an impressive new seven-and-a-half acre passenger and freight terminal for C.S.L. at Toronto. (The terminal included a special warehouse for storing the large shipments of peaches, grapes, and other fruits that the *Corona*, *Chippewa*, and *Cayuga* brought from the Niagara Peninsula.)

Sadly, both the Lewiston and Toronto piers would soon become underutilized as first one and then another C.S.L. passenger steamer was retired. The *Corona*, which in the 1920s had sailed for a few summers in C.S.L.'s service between Toronto and Hamilton, Ontario, until that was discontinued, returned late in the decade to the

Departure time nears for *Cayuga* at the then-new Toronto terminal. Judging by passengers' attire, they weren't escaping the heat. (C.S.L. photo, Marine Museum of the Great Lakes at Cayuga.)

The *Chippewa's* walking beam gets the once-over from an unidentified man. After she was retired, the steamer became shabby from neglect as this picture, taken at Toronto, attests. (Courtesy the Jay Bascom collection.)

Niagara route, only to be withdrawn for good at the end of the 1929 season. The *Chippewa* suffered the same fate at the close of the 1936 season. That left only the *Cayuga* to continue the Niagara service, and even she stopped calling at Lewiston after the 1938 season, terminating her voyages from Toronto thereafter only at Queenston.

While the drop-off in passenger traffic caused by the Great Depression undoubtedly contributed to C.S.L.'s decision to retire the boats, it also surely reflected the growing popularity of automobile travel. Indeed, the blossoming love affair Canadians and Americans had with their cars helps to explain the loss of convenient trolley and train services that brought passengers to the Niagara River piers. The interurban service from Niagara Falls to

the Queenston terminal ended in 1932 (a bus replaced it), and the electric-car line from the Falls to Lewiston never reopened after a rock-slide closed it in 1935. Earlier, the Michigan Central Railroad had discontinued passenger service from the Falls to the dock at Niagara-on-the-Lake (although it remained a port of call until the *Cayuga* stopped running).

The growth of auto travel might have doomed the *Cayuga* sooner had it not been for the outbreak of World War II. The war brought gas rationing and prompted pleasure-seeking Torontonians to forsake their cars in favour of the Niagara boat. "During the Second World War," writes Edgar Andrew Collard in his history of Canada Steamship Lines, "the *Cayuga* made more money for C.S.L. than any other ship the company owned."[7]

The steamer's stellar financial performance between 1940 and 1945 prompted the company to rebuild the *Cayuga* after the war ended. Improvements included the installation of new boilers fitted to burn oil, enabling her to switch from coal, a somewhat dirtier fuel. But the modernization of the ship failed to yield the returns the company had hoped for; after the *Cayuga* incurred a string of operating losses in the next few years, C.S.L. concluded late in 1951 that even under the most favourable conditions she couldn't break even.

"Victim of Rubber Tires" was the way *The* (Toronto) *Telegram* aptly headlined its article announcing that the company would retire the beloved vessel from service. The victim, however, was to get a reprieve.[8]

In 1953, a group of *Cayuga* fans, led by Alan Howard, a steamboat lover from Toronto, came forward to purchase from C.S.L. the laid-up ship along with the docks at Niagara-on-the-Lake and Queenston. The new owners, operating under the name Cayuga Steamship Co. Ltd., restored the vessel to her old run the following summer, with her smart appearance largely unchanged. The dark green hull colour she had sported for more than two decades had given way to black, and the iconic red, white, and black C.S.L. colours on her stacks had

given way to buff, silver, and black, but she was still instantly recognizable as the unfailingly graceful *Cayuga*.

Unfortunately, she encountered the same unrelenting economic headwinds under her new ownership that had buffeted her in her final years sailing for C.S.L. After the *Cayuga* pulled into Toronto's Pier Nine on Sept. 3, 1957, closing out yet another money-losing season, she never sailed again and was scrapped in the early 1960s.

Although the *Cayuga*'s career on Lake Ontario had spanned a half-century, for those who loved her she was still too young to die.

The *Cayuga*, as handsome as ever while operating for her last owners, Cayuga Steamship Co. Ltd., backs away from her Toronto pier in the 1950s. (Courtesy the Jay Bascom collection.)

CHAPTER 3

By Night Boat Through the Thousand Islands

I f you wanted to catch the choicest scenery on the next leg of the "Niagara to the Sea" journey, you had to arise early. Very early.

That's because C.S.L.'s overnight steamer from Toronto to Prescott, Ontario, would begin its voyage of more than two hours through the Thousand Islands of the St. Lawrence River around sunrise. It was the need to make connections with the company's Prescott-Montreal boat for the exciting daylight trip down the St. Lawrence rapids that dictated the less than optimal eastbound schedule of the boat through the islands. But the early arising apparently was well worth the effort: A C.S.L. brochure

likened this extraordinary archipelago (of 1,692 isles to be precise) to "a marvelous array of jewels … some of them emerald with their trees and woods, others bare masses of rock cut into strange shapes, and others gay with house and lawn and garden." It continued: "Every turn of the channel that divides the islands is fascinating, with the bright light of the summer morning to enhance the charm."[1]

Preparing for another summer season are, from left, Kingston; Cayuga, *whose two stacks are partly visible; and* Toronto. *The date is May 4, 1931. (Courtesy the Jay Bascom collection.)*

Right: Here's the *Toronto* as she appeared when operating for the Richelieu and Ontario Navigation Co., her original owner. Side poles for flags were commonplace on inland and coastal passenger steamers at the turn of the twentieth century; most ships, including the *Toronto*, eventually were stripped of this decorative touch. (C.S.L. photo, Marine Museum of the Great Lakes at Kingston.)

Below: The *Kingston* never looked better than when she was all white with ornate trailboards still adorning her bows. She's seen here, probably in the 1920s, departing Toronto Harbour. (Courtesy the Jay Bascom collection.)

Another company publication, employing less florid prose, noted that about half the islands are in Canada, being mostly as nature made them, and that the other half, in U.S. waters, support "some of the most beautiful and luxurious summer homes in America." The stretch of the St. Lawrence near the steamer stop at Alexandria Bay, New York, was especially scenic, narrow enough that a special pilot was required to navigate it and so enticing that some of the best-known millionaires in the nation built their houses along it.[2]

When passengers who had embarked at Toronto the previous afternoon reached the C.S.L. dock at Prescott, they would have been aboard their steamer for sixteen hours.

In that time, she would have crossed Lake Ontario to Charlotte, (Rochester) New York, arriving there to pick up additional passengers at 9 p.m. or 10 p.m. depending on the year, and then re-crossed the lake to Kingston, Ontario, during the night before heading for the Thousand Islands and then Prescott. This was a route from which the two wonderful paddlewheel ships that C.S.L. operated on it — the *Toronto* of 1899 and the *Kingston* of 1901 — never deviated in their entire (and blessedly long) careers.

Launched for Richelieu and Ontario Navigation Co., both ships were designed by Arendt Angstrom, the man responsible for the fine lines of the *Corona* and *Cayuga* on

The beauty of the *Kingston* was more than skin deep, as evidenced by this circa-1904 view of her main saloon. (Notman photo, VIEW-6544 McCord Museum, Montreal.)

the Niagara run. The same feel for proportion he demonstrated with those vessels was evident in the *Toronto* and *Kingston*, which remind steamboat connoisseurs of the splendid paddlewheel night boats once operated by the illustrious Fall River Line between New York City and Fall River, Massachusetts. (The similarity isn't surprising; before joining Toronto's Bertram Iron Works, which built the two Toronto-Prescott steamers, Angstrom had worked under George Pierce, the naval architect for some of the Fall River's most admired vessels.)

My preference is for the *Toronto*, which sported a single thick stack that gave her a better-balanced profile than the slightly larger *Kingston*, with her two rather spindly stacks. Two prominent ventilators on the *Kingston's* promenade deck forward of the cabins — a feature that the *Toronto*, fortunately, lacked — did nothing to enhance her appearance. Both boats, though, did Angstrom proud. Each possessed one of the handsome pilothouses for which he was noted, each had beautiful gilded trailboards gracing their bows (that were to disappear with the passage of time), and each had remarkably refined public rooms that must have been an uplifting sight to embarking passengers.

The *Kingston* was particularly renowned for her interior décor, and Donald Page, a former C.S.L. executive who researched the histories of the company's ships, tells why in an article he wrote some years ago. "The light and spacious three-decked superstructure which housed the passengers," he recounted, "... was a spectacular display of domed and frescoed ceilings, Corinthian columns, curving staircases and potted palms... Excellent meals were served in the splendid, paneled dining salon." (In contrast, he noted, the individual passenger

cabins were rather austere, with an upper and lower berth, a washbasin, and a single chair in each one.)[3]

The two ships operated daily during the summer months, one sailing east from Toronto and the other west from Prescott, the *Toronto* with approximately 330 berths, the *Kingston* with 365. While the eastbound trip might disappoint slugabeds, who would miss much of the Thousand Islands scenery because of the early hour, the westbound voyage afforded a chance to see the archipelago entirely by daylight. The boats left Prescott in the early afternoon and passed the last of the islands a little over four hours later. After stops at Kingston and Charlotte (Rochester), the westbound steamer would arrive in Toronto the next morning before the start of the business day.

For decades, the two boats stopped on their route through the Thousand Islands not only at Alexandria Bay but also at Clayton, New York, an important port of call because of its role as a terminus for the New York Central Railroad. During the summer, the railroad offered special sleeping car service from Boston, New York, and Chicago directly to the steamer wharf there.

Patronage on the Toronto-Prescott route was great enough in the first decade of C.S.L. control that in October 1924 the company's directors authorized the expenditure of up to $500,000 — serious money back then — for the lengthening of the 281-foot-long *Toronto* by forty feet and "the complete rearrangement and modernizing of the stateroom accommodation thereon, provided that this entire improvement can be completed on or before the opening of the 1925 season of navigation."[4] The planned upgrade, which would have made the *Toronto* longer than the *Kingston*, was abandoned after C.S.L. determined that the deadline could not be met.

It is questionable, however, whether such a project, if it had been completed, would have paid for itself in a reasonable amount of time. Even in the last years of the Roaring Twenties, C.S.L.'s overall passenger traffic had begun to decline, and after the onset of the Great Depression it went into free fall. Although business overall had improved by the mid-1930s, the Toronto-Prescott service itself was scaled back a bit: Clayton, the longtime New York Central terminus, had been eliminated as a steamer stop by then.

A short while later, the Toronto-Prescott service received another setback in the form of more stringent U.S. maritime safety regulations. Prompted by the disastrous fire in 1934 aboard the U.S. coastal passenger ship *Morro Castle*, the regulations, which would take effect in 1938, included a ban on the

operation of passenger steamers in American waters with a wooden main deck, which the *Toronto* had. (The *Kingston*, which had a steel main deck, was unaffected.)

The increasingly inhospitable economic climate for steamboats — it had already prompted C.S.L. to retire two of its three vessels on the Niagara run — could only have stiffened the company's resolve not to sink more money into the *Toronto* to bring her into compliance. And so, after she had finished the 1937 season, C.S.L. laid her up. The pretty paddler would never run again, and the only other voyage she would make was to a scrapyard a decade later.

With only the *Kingston* remaining on the Toronto-Prescott route, service was reduced to three sailings a week in each direction. Ironically, had the *Toronto* been able to continue operating into the early 1940s, there

Fortunately, the proposed lengthening of *Toronto* (by forty feet) never materialized. Judging from this photo, taken in the Thousand Islands, her proportions were perfect already. (C.S.L. photo, Marine Museum of the Great Lakes.)

SS. Kingston

probably would have been plenty of business for both vessels, since wartime gasoline rationing encouraged people to take their vacation on a steamer instead of in a car.

For a time, C.S.L. remained undecided about its plans for improving service on the route, by now reduced to one forty-year-old ship. Coverdale, then the company's president, stressed at a 1941 directors meeting the difficulty in providing up-to-date passenger service on Lake Ontario and the St. Lawrence River west of Montreal with the ships available — meaning the *Kingston* on the Toronto-Prescott segment and the *Rapids Prince* on the Prescott-Montreal segment — owing to uncertainty about what he called "the St. Lawrence Deep-Waterways Scheme."[5]

He was, of course, referring to a long-advocated plan to build what would become known as the St. Lawrence Seaway, a canal system on the St. Lawrence River capable of accommodating much larger

vessels than the system used by ships for generations before the Seaway opened in 1959. Coverdale was right to be cautious: completion of the project, which included construction of a dam across the upper St. Lawrence for power generation, made it impossible for ships to continue to run the

(Bibliothèque et Archives nationales du Québec collection Magella Bureau P547. S2.553.D3.P662.)

rapids all the way between Prescott and Montreal. And for C.S.L. the demise of its rapids service would have threatened the viability of its Toronto-Prescott service, since so many passengers used it to connect with the *Rapids Prince*.

It's unclear from C.S.L.'s board-meeting records for the period what changed Coverdale's mind about building a replacement for the *Kingston*, but by 1944 he was fully committed to it. Two years later, by which time the war had ended, sketchy details about the new ship could be gleaned from the corporate records: She would be built at C.S.L.'s shipyard in Kingston "along similar lines to the *S.S. Tadoussac*," launched in 1928 for the company's Montreal-Quebec-City-Saguenay service.[6] Basing the design of a new ship on one that old seems, in retrospect, an example of going "back to the future."

Indeed, C.S.L. may have had second thoughts about the design. An artist's depiction of the planned new vessel that was featured in company brochures of the late 1940s showed a ship bearing scant resemblance to the *Tadoussac*. Whereas that steamer had a very traditional profile, with a straight stem and two stacks, the proposed new boat had a modern raked prow and a single, streamlined funnel. By one account, from 1945, she was to be approximately 320 feet long, or about twenty feet longer than the *Kingston*.

In what would have been a radical departure for C.S.L., the new ship was designed to sail the Great Lakes and St. Lawrence in summer and cruise to the West Indies from Miami in the winter, Donald Page, who was an official at the Kingston shipyard in the 1940s, would write many years later. If she had been completed with a length of 320 feet, the steamer would have been confined for about the first decade of her existence to the Toronto-Prescott run, since she would have been too long to use the existing St. Lawrence canal system.

In this 1920s scene, *Cape Trinity* is clearing Toronto Harbour as Canadian National Steamers' excursion vessel *Dalhousie City* returns from a voyage to Port Dalhousie, ON. (Courtesy the Jay Bascom collection.)

THE ALSO-RANS

The *Toronto* and *Kingston* weren't the only overnight steamers that Canada Steamship Lines operated between Lake Ontario and the St. Lawrence River.

During its first decade and a half, the company also employed two smallish propeller-driven night boats on the lake and river that had much shorter (and decidedly less successful) careers with C.S.L. than the two-paddle wheelers on the Toronto-Prescott run.

One of the propeller boats, built in 1911 for the Ontario and Quebec Navigation Co. as the *Geronia*, was designed to run all the way from Toronto to Montreal and had protective wooden sheathing over her steel hull for shooting the rapids of the St. Lawrence below Prescott. After that company was acquired in 1913 by C.S.L., it renamed the 230-foot-long single-stack vessel *Syracuse* and put her on a route between Lewiston, New York, on the Niagara River, and Ogdensburg, New York, on the St. Lawrence opposite Prescott. Her running mate on the route was a 256-foot-long twin-funnelled ship called the *Rochester*, completed in 1910 for the Richelieu and Ontario Navigation Co. of the United States, which, like the parent Canadian-based R. & O. company, became part of Canada Steamship at its inception. As it turned out, C.S.L. never found the right niche for these two ships.

Within a few years, C.S.L. moved the steamers to its Montreal-Quebec City-Saguenay route, renaming the *Syracuse* the *Cape Trinity* and the *Rochester* the *Cape Eternity* to honour the two most stunning topographical features of the Saguenay River. But by 1923, the *Cape Trinity* was back on Lake Ontario and the upper St. Lawrence, sailing between Toronto and Prescott, although on a somewhat different route from the *Toronto* and the *Kingston*. Unlike those ships, she called only at Alexandria Bay, New York, on her eastbound trips and stopped only at Ontario ports — Kingston and Belleville, on the scenic Bay of Quinte — on her westbound trips.

The *Cape Trinity* was withdrawn after the conclusion of the 1928 season and scrapped. The *Cape Eternity* remained longer on the Montreal-Saguenay route but she, too, had returned to Lake Ontario by the late 1920s, reportedly mainly running charter trips there. She made just three trips in 1931 and never ran again for C.S.L. (It sold the *Cape Eternity* to a company that operated her as the *Georgian* in the late 1930s and early 1940s between Windsor and ports on Georgian Bay. She was sold to a Chinese firm after World War II.)

It's unlikely that many steamboat lovers mourned the disappearance of the rather ungainly *Capes* from the C.S.L. roster. In fact, the marine historian Jay Bascom has called them "two of the most unlovely overnight passenger boats to operate in the Lake Ontario area during this century."[7]

But any consideration of a new vessel ceased when C.S.L. decided in late 1949 to end service on both the Toronto-Prescott and rapids routes after two pivotal events earlier that year — the death of Coverdale, the leading proponent of the new ship, and the tragic fire aboard its Upper Lakes passenger steamer *Noronic*, which led to new safety regulations so costly that the company couldn't afford to retrofit the *Kingston* to make her comply. (As it was, the Toronto-Prescott and rapids services had lost money for the five previous seasons.)

When the *Kingston* was towed to a scrapyard in 1950, it brought to an end 110 years of continuous passenger service between Lake Ontario and the St. Lawrence River. It was, as they say, nice while it lasted.

The *Cape Eternity* visits Tadoussac while employed on C.S.L.'s Montreal-Saguenay service in the 1920s. (C.S.L. photo, Marine Museum of the Great Lakes at Kingston.)

CHAPTER 4

Running the Rapids

If steaming down the St. Lawrence River past the Thousand Islands failed to arouse the enthusiasm of some passengers, Canada Steamship Lines had a surefire treat for them later the same day.

That would come after travellers embarked on the third segment of their "Niagara to the Sea" journey at Prescott, Ontario, for a nine-and-a-half-hour trip to Montreal aboard a vessel specially designed for what the company called "the fastest water navigable by steamships."[1] Ahead lay

For four decades, the *Rapids Prince* thrilled passengers as she ran the treacherous Lachine Rapids of the St. Lawrence, shown here. (Library and Archives Canada/Hayward Studios fonds/PA-078547.)

a series of rapids in the St. Lawrence so turbulent that only C.S.L. passenger steamers sailed them; all the other commercial craft on the river bypassed them, using canals instead. Guess which route was more exciting?

There were eight sets of rapids in the approximately 130 miles between Prescott and Montreal, but there were two sets in particular that took passengers' breath away. One of these, the Long Sault Rapids, came early in the trip. Mervyn Allan Sayer, who made the steamer voyage in the late 1940s, wrote about the experience of coming upon "a seething mass of white churning water. As we approach, the engines are stopped, and the ship drifts with the current alone, faster and faster into the first mile, which contains treacherous reefs. We are now traveling at between twenty and as high as thirty miles per hour. The downward and undulating motion gives you a peculiar sensation. This is caused by the vessel actually dropping down the hill of water."[2]

Even more exciting were the Lachine Rapids, which the steamer encountered shortly before reaching Montreal. Whereas she had dropped forty-five feet over nine miles in the Long Sault Rapids, in the Lachine she descended fifty-six feet in just two miles. Here's how C.S.L. described that adventure: "The channel through the Lachine Rapids is narrow and tortuous. In plunges the steamer among the breakers, and the headlong current carries her on towards the insidious rocks, sometimes hidden, sometimes exposed to view, with the dark suggestion of others unseen below the waters; deftly the steamer passes them by, within a few feet of their treacherous edges, through clouds of spray ascending from the churning abyss."[3]

To minimize damage to the steamers, their steel hulls were sheathed with a thick protective layer of wood to soften the impact should they scrape rocks while navigating the rapids.

Not surprisingly, given the potential for disaster that lurked in the rapids, C.S.L. hired special pilots to take its steamers through them. It was a job so demanding that only successive generations of one family reportedly were permitted to perform it. "It's either my uncle or myself," one of the pilots, Capt. Joseph Ouellette, once told The (Montreal) *Gazette*. "We are the only ones qualified to make the run."[4]

Passengers presumably must have appreciated C.S.L.'s attentiveness to their needs on the rapids trip. After a reconstruction of two of the boats in 1929, a company brochure boasted, "These steamers have been entirely rebuilt in order to provide the maximum amount of deck space so that every passenger may be assured of perfect views … whether from within, through the wide-vision windows of the spacious glass-enclosed observation deck, or from the equally spacious decks outside. A special feature is a comfortable armchair for every passenger, those of the enclosed deck being of the upholstered, wicker type."[5]

In the early C.S.L. years, the eastbound rapids boat left Prescott in mid-morning and arrived in Montreal in early evening; the steamer would then make a more leisurely return trip to Prescott using the canals. (Until the late 1920s, the ships would carry passengers in both directions. Thereafter, the westbound boat carried only her crew, while travellers took a train from Montreal to Prescott to connect there with C.S.L's night boat to Toronto.)

It paid to arrive early at the bow of a rapids steamer if you wanted the best vantage point for the turbulent waters ahead. (Credit: C.S.L. photo, Marine Museum of the Great Lakes at Kingston.)

Right: *Rapids Queen* lies at rest about 1925 at Montreal's Victoria Pier, home base for C.S.L.'s rapids steamers. (Notman archives, MP-0000.25.213, McCord Museum, Montreal.)

Below: The Soulanges Canal, pictured here, was one of a series of canals that steamers would use to bypass the rapids of the St. Lawrence on their return trip from Montreal. (Notman archives, M2004.117.15.4, McCord Museum, Montreal.)

By the time C.S.L. inherited the rapids service from Richelieu and Ontario Navigation Co., in 1913, it was being performed by three propeller-driven steamers, the *Rapids Queen*, the *Rapids King*, and the *Rapids Prince*. Two of the three rapids vessels would serve C.S.L. quite well, while the third would prove a chronic disappointment.

The *Rapids Queen* was one of the successful boats. Built for the R. and O. at Chester, Pennsylvania, in 1892 as the single-stack *Columbian*, she was twice renamed and rebuilt. It was in the second upgrade, in 1909, that the vessel received her royal nomenclature, as well as an increase in her length (to 210 feet) and an additional stack. The two nearly perpendicular funnels, combined with a minimal sheer (or curvature of the hull from bow to stern), gave her a somewhat awkward appearance. Handsome or not, she operated for another two decades on the rapids run and wasn't retired from it until 1929.

Niagara to the Sea

Shooting the Rapids

THE most satisfying trip in America for health and recreation. Almost 1000 miles of lakes, rivers and rapids, including the Thousand Islands, the exciting descent of the marvelous rapids, the historic associations of Montreal, Quaint old Quebec, with its famous miracle-working Shrine of Ste. Anne de Beaupré and the renowned Saguenay River, with its stupendous Capes, "Trinity" and "Eternity," higher than Gibraltar.

Send 2c postage for illustrated booklet, "Niagara to the Sea," including map and guide, to JOHN F. PIERCE, Pass. Traffic Manager, Canada Steamship Lines, Ltd., 115 C. S. L. Building, Montreal, Canada.

CANADA STEAMSHIP LINES

Below: This picture of the *Rapids King,* taken as she was shooting the Lachine Rapids in her original Richelieu and Ontario Navigation Co. colours, was used for decades by C.S.L. to promote its rapids steamers. (Notman photo, VIEW-4271, McCord Museum, Montreal.)

More aesthetically pleasing was the single-stack *Rapids King* of 1907, which was built in Canada and designed by Arendt Angstrom, creator of the esteemed *Toronto* and *Kingston* for the R&O's Toronto-Prescott service. Because of a design flaw, however, the *Rapids King* proved poorly suited to whatever role she served. Although a ship needed to draw no more than six feet of water if she were to safely navigate the Long Sault and Lachine Rapids, the *Rapids King*, incomprehensibly, drew six and a half feet, which meant that she frequently ran aground. When C.S.L. shifted her in the 1920s to a service out of Detroit, her lightweight construction caused her to roll badly in open water and she was laid up for more than a year.

Finally, in the winter of 1929, C.S.L. decided to further reduce the ship's weight so as to reduce her draft enough that she could return to the rapids route. The measures taken included removing the forward part of her promenade deck, stripping all cabins from her upper deck — the rapids steamers, though day boats, originally had a limited number of private staterooms —

and converting her from a coal-burning to an oil-burning vessel. The modifications, however, came on the eve of the Great Depression, and the *Rapids King* was laid up in the early 1930s at Sorel, Quebec, and never sailed again. She was sold for scrap in 1949.

The *Rapids Prince* of 1910, which received a similar downsizing at the same time as the *Rapids King,* had a much happier career and was the longest serving of the three boats. Like that steamer, the *Rapids Prince* was built at Toronto and designed by Angstrom, who gave her a flattering slightly raked stem, a single stack of just the right thickness and, overall, near-perfect proportions. That she was thirty-five feet shorter than the earlier boat and drew only five feet of water made her less likely to run aground in the rapids. (Even so, the *Rapids Prince* wasn't immune to groundings; one that occurred in 1922 in the Lachine Rapids after she broke a rudder chain put her out of service for all of August and part of September. Another grounding, caused by pilot error, in the same rapids left the ship stranded in the river for more than two and a half months in the summer of 1941.)

During the last two decades of the service, passengers weren't always able to savour the complete rapids experience. For example, because of low water in the Lachine Rapids, the most exciting part of the eastbound trip, the *Rapids Prince* was unable to navigate them for five seasons beginning in 1934. In those years, she took passengers only as far as Lachine Wharf, where they transferred to buses that carried them to Victoria Pier in Montreal, the departure point for C.S.L. steamers to Quebec City and the Saguenay River. What disappointment those travellers must have felt!

Mervyn Allan Sayer, who produced his account of the rapids trip for *Australian Power Boat and Yachting Monthly Magazine,* reported that until 1940 the *Rapids Prince* ran the Coteau, Cedar, Split Rock, Cascades, and Soulanges Rapids on her way down the river. "This section of the river was then closed to navigation with the building of the huge power plants in this area," he wrote. The steamer bypassed those rapids, taking the parallel 15-mile-long Soulanges Canal instead.[6]

What remained of the eastbound trip right to the end, however, were its very best segments, the running of the Long Sault and Lachine Rapids, which the *Rapids Prince* did on her last day of service, September 18, 1949, with an Ouellette as pilot. The steamer was scrapped in 1951, fittingly, where the *Kingston,* of the connecting Toronto-Prescott route, met her demise the previous year.

CHAPTER 5

To Saltwater and the "Sentinels" of the Saguenay

It was the final leg of the "Niagara to the Sea" trip that Canada Steamship Lines passengers probably relished most of all. For they could hardly help being charmed by a voyage that combined the exquisite scenery of the Montreal-Quebec City-Saguenay route with a dash of French-Canadian culture.

Those attractions and the splendid ships that brought people to them — the newest and largest ships in the fleet — help to explain why this was C.S.L.'s longest lasting passenger service and likely its most fondly remembered one.

The voyage down the St. Lawrence would begin from Montreal's Victoria Pier around 6:30 p.m, a departure timed so that passengers could enjoy the ever-changing views while eating in their steamer's spacious dining room, with its large observation windows. Later, perhaps after dancing to the ship's orchestra, travellers would retire for the night to their stateroom as she continued her eleven-and-a-half-hour voyage to storied Quebec City. Could there have been a better way to appreciate the majesty of the onetime capital of New France — with its iconic Upper and Lower Towns —than from the deck of a C.S.L. ship at daybreak? I doubt it.

The ship would spend about two hours there before resuming her voyage down the St. Lawrence. Benny Beattie lovingly recalled what came next from his many trips over the route. "After leaving Quebec City," he writes in his book *Tadoussac: The Sands of Summer*, Beattie and his family would head for a breakfast in the ship's dining room that included "creamy porridge with a fine powdery sugar, hot pancakes with maple syrup, grilled sausages with ham and bacon and eggs [and] steaming hot corn and bran muffins."[1] Fortified with such fare, passengers might then feast their eyes on the achingly beautiful vistas unfolding before them on the lower St. Lawrence. Here's a word picture painted in a C.S.L. brochure:

"After passing the southern shore of the Isle of Orleans, our steamer follows the north shore of the river … The mountainous capes and bold banks of the river delight the eye with every shade and blend of color, whilst the health-restoring odors from the pine, spruce and cedar [trees] impregnate the salt air with their wholesome fragrance." And it gets better.

Right: This 1917 ad shows one of C.S.L.'s two paddle-wheelers then operating the Montreal-Quebec overnight service sailing past the august Chateau Frontenac hotel en route to the company's wharf in Quebec's Lower Town. (Author's collection.)

Arriving at Historic Quebec

On one of the magnificent steamers on the route

Niagara to the Sea

The all-water trip to Montreal, Quebec and the Saguenay River by the steamers of the Canada Steamship Lines is one of the grandest trips in America for health and recreation.

The mighty heroes of North America are no more but Quebec, cradle of New France, where they walked and talked still survives; quaint, historic, ancient; majestic in its beauty and isolation.

Every hour of the 1000 mile journey has its revelation of beauty, grandeur and historic interest—Niagara, the most sublime of all nature's handiwork, Toronto, "The Queen City of Canada," the fairylike Thousand Islands of the St. Lawrence, the thrilling descent of the marvelous rapids, the great Canadian Metropolis Montreal, the miracle-working shrine of Ste. Anne de Beaupré just an hour from Quebec, the stupendous Capes "Trinity" and "Eternity"—higher than Gibraltar—on the Saguenay River are all on this route. Up-to-date Canada Steamship hotels at Murray Bay and Tadousac.

A thousand miles of travel—A thousand thrills of pleasure

FARES FROM NIAGARA FALLS:

To Montreal and return - - - - -	$19.00
To Quebec and return - - - - -	26.35
To Saguenay River and return - - - -	35.00

Send 2c postage for illustrated booklet, map and guide to JOHN F. PIERCE, Asst. Pass. Traffic Manager, Canada Steamship Lines, 165 R. & O. Bldg., Montreal, Canada.

CANADA STEAMSHIP LINES

Shooting the Famous rapids of the St. Lawrence

A photograph for a
C.S.L. brochure, taken
from the hurricane
deck of the *Richelieu*,
suggests the fine
scenery that awaited
passengers on the
Montreal-Saguenay
route. (Cover of
Saguenay travel log,
Hoopes donation,
Musée de Charlevoix.)

"Mount Ste. Anne, 2,700 feet in height … is seen in passing the east end of the Isle of Orleans, and a short distance beyond is Cape Tourmente, 2,000 feet in height. Here, saltwater begins, and the river widens until it assumes the proportion of an inland sea." (It will broaden to fifteen miles in a couple of hours.)[2]

Not all the interesting scenery was stationary, of course. Part of the fun was watching passing ships at close range, particularly the handsome transatlantic passenger liners en route to Quebec and Montreal or Europe. Foremost among them were vessels of the Cunard Line and Canadian Pacific's white Empresses and, in the interwar years, also its "Mont" and "Duchess" ships. In short, the river was a ship-lover's delight.

Until 1931, C.S.L. steamers would stop at four small river communities of considerable charm in the stunning Charlevoix region of Quebec province — Baie-Saint-Paul, Les Éboulements, Saint-Irénée, and Cap à l'Aigle. But beginning that year, the number of stops in Charlevoix was cut back

to two, Murray Bay (now La Malbaie) and Saint-Simeon. There was never any danger that Murray Bay would be eliminated since it was the site of the company's grand, chateau-inspired hotel, the Manoir Riche-lieu, where many passengers were headed. It was, after all, the social hub of what C.S.L. touted as "Canada's most exclusive summer resort."[3]

From the stop at Saint-Simeon, farther downriver, the boat steamed for Tadoussac, the first permanent French settlement in North America and the site of another, less formal C.S.L. hostelry, the Hotel Tadoussac. After an hour stopover there, the ship would leave the St. Lawrence and head into a tributary — the incomparable, fjord-like Saguenay River — that most passengers surely would have agreed was the scenic highpoint of their trip.

How scenic? Benny Beattie writes of the "savage strength of the Saguenay," with its "massive mountains"[4] — part of the Lauren-tians, reputedly the oldest range in North America — and water that's "dark blue, almost purple."[5] An early C.S.L. brochure

was more detailed: "Cut through the mountains by glacial action, this awesome river, its waters more than 700 feet in depth, has a solemn grandeur common to no other stream, its banks towering above the dark waters … rugged and precipitous and, for the most part, cliffs of solid granite."[6]

C.S.L. steamers would take three and a half hours or so to cruise the Saguenay from Tadoussac to Bagotville, where they would spend the night before heading back to Montreal; the company's deluxe cruise ship *Richelieu* often sailed farther up the river, to the head of navigation, Chicoutimi ("Up to Here Is Deep" in a First Nations dialect), some sixty miles upriver. Easily the most memorable topographical features of the cruise were Capes Trinity and Eternity. These "twin sentinels" of the Saguenay, as C.S.L. called them, were backdrops for steamer photos in nearly all the promotional material for the route, and you can understand why.

Rising nearly perpendicularly from the water to heights described as anywhere from 1,500 feet to 1,800 feet, depending on what source you're consulting, the two

The Tadoussac, brimming with passengers on deck, leaves the St. Lawrence (left) and enters the mouth of the Saguenay River at Tadoussac. ("Tadoussac dans la baie," Musée de Charlevoix.)

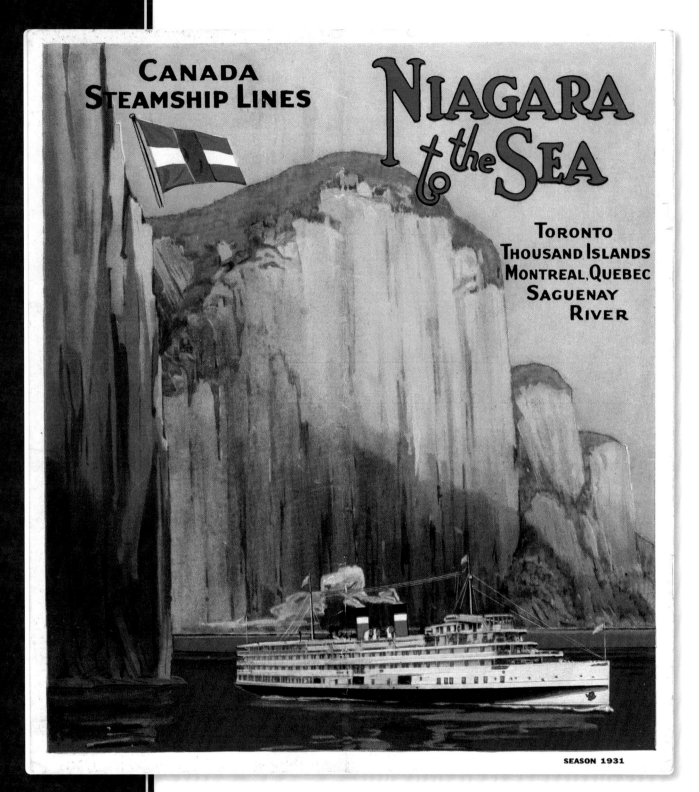

CANADA STEAMSHIP LINES

NIAGARA to the SEA

TORONTO
THOUSAND ISLANDS
MONTREAL, QUEBEC
SAGUENAY
RIVER

SEASON 1931

Towering capes of the Saguenay form the backdrop for the *St. Lawrence* on the cover of the 1931 brochure. (Author's collection.)

capes were truly awesome; one C.S.L. brochure said that when a steamer hugs the base of Cape Trinity, "it appears as if it might fall over and crush" her. Adding to the drama was the reverberation of a ship's whistle blast as it was echoed and re-echoed by the mighty promontories.[7]

Passengers who made the round-trip to the Saguenay spent three nights aboard their ship, a schedule that enabled someone in Montreal to board a steamer after work on Friday and return there on Monday before the start of the business day, having taken a magnificent cruise covering more than 700 miles. (At times, C.S.L. also offered more leisurely six-day cruises on the route — first with the *Cape Eternity* in the 1920s and later with the *Richelieu* — that involved overnight stopovers at Tadoussac and Murray Bay.)

In the early years after it inherited the Montreal-Saguenay route from the Richelieu and Ontario Navigation Co., C.S.L. operated two intriguing paddle-wheelers solely on the overnight Montreal-Quebec City service and used other steamers for

the Saguenay service. The two paddlers were named, appropriately, *Montreal* and *Quebec*. Though they were running mates for more than two decades, they had very different histories.

The *Montreal*, another beauty designed for the R. & O. by Arendt Angstrom, the naval architect responsible for the aforementioned *Toronto, Kingston, Rapids King,* and *Rapids Prince,* was really a larger rendition of the *Kingston* of the Toronto-Prescott overnight service. Like that handsome vessel, the *Montreal*, which debuted in 1905, had two stacks (albeit more raked and substantial looking than the *Kingston's*), elegant gilded trailboards at her bow, and wonderfully opulent public spaces. Perhaps her most distinctive interior feature was a portrait above one of the ship's grand staircases of Cardinal Richelieu by the distinguished French-Canadian artist Marc-Aurele de Foy Suzor-Coté. For good reason, the *Montreal*, the biggest boat ever built for the R.&O., has been called its "crowning glory."[8]

(Credit: Hoopes donation, Musée de Charlevoix.)

PRINTED IN CANADA.

CANADA STEAMSHIP LINES LIMITED

MONTREAL, Que.

TO—A

Saguenay River-Rivière Saguenay

AND RETURN   ET RETOUR

Meals and Berth included—Repas et Lit inclus.

Form Sag. Exc. 5   86567

Follow the Trail of the Heroes of Old

MIGHTY MEN were they who followed the fleur-de-lis of France and the banner of St. George of Old England up the sparkling waters of the St. Lawrence—Cartier, Frontenac, La Salle, Hennepin, Wolfe and other immortal heroes.

A voyage to old Quebec, and on through the stupendous gorge of the Saguenay, is an experience unforgettable. From the decks of modern, luxurious steamships of the Canada Steamship Lines, this land of romance and adventure is yours to re-discover. Thousands have thrilled to the magic of the mighty St. Lawrence—"The Greatest River without Comparison that is known to have ever been seen," as Cartier wrote to his King, nearly four hundred years ago.

Look at the map. You can begin your journey at Niagara Falls, Toronto, Rochester, Alexandria Bay, Clayton, Montreal or Quebec, and return the same way; arranging your trip so as to stop off a day at the important points without having to worry about hotel accommodations.

Send 2c in stamps for illustrated booklet, map and guide, "Niagara to the Sea," to John F. Pierce, Passenger Traffic Mgr., Canada Steamship Lines, Ltd , 109 C.S.L. Bldg., Montreal, Canada.

"Niagara to the Sea"

A Thousand Miles of Travel
A Thousand Thrills of Pleasure

CANADA STEAMSHIP LINES

The *Quebec*, unlike her homegrown counterpart, was built in Scotland, knocked down for transport aboard a transatlantic ship, and then reassembled in Canada. She predated the *Montreal* by forty years, but three major makeovers in as many decades enabled the older boat to be a suitable sister ship for the newer one. In her final reconstruction, in 1907, the *Quebec* was lengthened to 311 overall — just twenty-nine feet shorter than the *Montreal* — and given a totally new superstructure that made her look like a slightly smaller version of the larger boat. (Like her running mate, the *Quebec* carried two stacks.)

By 1920 passenger traffic on the Montreal-Quebec City route had grown to where the *Quebec* lacked sufficient capacity to handle it. C.S.L. directors were considering putting the steamer, then in her fifty-fifth year, on the less demanding Saguenay service and buying a replacement for the run between the two cities. Although the company's president, J.W. Norcoss, acknowledged that the ideal replacement would be a new ship built to C.S.L.'s specifications, he said that reconditioning an existing boat would be cheaper and faster.

Left: The ad's creator exercised some artistic license in depicting what's unmistakably the *Montreal* sailing past the capes of the Saguenay; as it happened, the elegant steamer never proceeded east of Quebec City. (Author's collection.)

Above: It would be hard to improve on the proportions of the *Montreal*, shown here in her original Richelieu and Ontario livery. (Her stacks were painted crimson with a black band at the top.) (Notman photo VIEW-6562.0 McCord Museum, Montreal.)

Above: The transfer of ownership of the *Montreal* from the Richelieu and Ontario Navigation Co. to C.S.L. did nothing to spoil her splendid appearance, as this picture proves. (Photo published in 1992 "Les Bateaux Blancs" issue of *Le Carignan* by Société historique Pierre-de-Saurel SHPS_20110419-001.)

Below: In this panoramic view of Quebec's Lower Town, the *Montreal* lies at the C.S.L. dock as the ferry *Lauzon* departs for Levis on the south shore of the St. Lawrence. (C.S.L. photo, Marine Museum of the Great Lakes at Kingston.)

So, within a few months, Norcross had concluded a deal to buy from the U.S. government the *S.S. Narragansett*, a two-stacked propeller-driven passenger steamer of approximately the same size and capacity as the *Montreal*. Built at Wilmington, Delaware, in 1913 to operate between New York City and Providence, Rhode Island, the *Narragansett* never saw service on that route and lay idle until requisitioned for transporting troops on the English Channel after America entered World War I.

Norcross assured fellow members of C.S.L.'s executive committee that his acquisition represented a very good value. The cost of the purchase and the reconditioning was projected to be no greater than $600,000. As it turned out, the total bill was

A portrait of Cardinal Richelieu by the noted Quebec artist Marc-Aurèle de Foy Suzor-Coté greeted passengers on the *Montreal*. The painting was transferred to the *Richelieu* in time for her debut on the Montre-al-Saguenay service in 1923. (Notman photo, VIEW-6560.0, McCord Museum, Montreal.)

Above: C.S.L.'s first *Quebec*, built in 1865, underwent three major reconstructions while under the ownership of Richelieu and Ontario Navigation Co. Here she is in one of her earlier incarnations. (Notman photo, VIEW-2477.A, McCord Museum, Montreal.)

Below: Pictured here in C.S.L. colours at Victoria Pier, Montreal, the *Quebec* was longer and sleeker after her third and final makeover and, thus, a more suitable running mate for the *Montreal*. Modernizing touches during the *Quebec*'s last reconstruction included concealment of her old-fashioned walking beam in dummy cabins abaft her stacks. The *Rapids Prince* is astern of her. (C.S.L. photo, Marine Museum of the Great Lakes at Kingston.)

twice that, and the reconditioning of the steamer — renamed *Richelieu* by C.S.L. — wasn't completed until the spring of 1923, two years after the company bought her. Nor did she become the *Montreal's* running mate on the Montreal-Quebec City line; the old *Quebec* would continue to play that role for another few years.

Instead, the *Richelieu* entered the company's increasingly popular service to the Saguenay, where she would operate until C.S.L. for most of the forty-two years she served the company. A particularly pleasing feature of the steamer, added during her reconstruction, was the fitting of many staterooms with their own verandahs. These deluxe staterooms, the company boasted, afforded their occupants the opportunity to view scenery without having to go on the deck and offered "absolute privacy."[9]

Several trips by Norcross on C.S.L.'s Montreal-Quebec City steamers had persuaded him of the need for this amenity. His observation, recorded at a 1921 board meeting, was that a great many staterooms on those steamers — meaning the *Montreal*

and *Quebec* — had windows opening on the deck, where passengers sat up late talking and disturbing the sleep of other passengers. On the *Richelieu*, the private verandahs would solve that problem.

Before the *Richelieu* joined the Saguenay service, C.S.L. had been operating it mainly with steamers designed for other routes. Each of these ships seemed to have a serious defect. Some were too elderly — like the *Tadousac* (1879), *Cape Diamond* (1877), and *Cape St. Francis* (1867) — while the more modern propeller-driven *Cape Trinity*

From an aesthetic standpoint, the *Richelieu*, shown here soon after she began sailing for C.S.L., was unprepossessing. The stowage of lifeboats on her hurricane deck made her look too high for her length, and her stacks looked too short for her height. (S.J. Hayward photo, Musée de Charlevoix.)

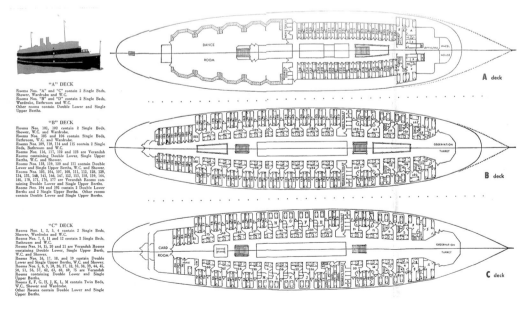

"A" DECK
Rooms Nos. "A" and "C" contain 2 Single Beds, Shower, Wardrobe and W.C.
Rooms Nos. "B" and "D" contain 2 Single Beds, Wardrobe, Bathroom and W.C.
Other rooms contain Double Lower and Single Upper Berths.

"B" DECK
Rooms Nos. 101, 102 contain 2 Single Beds, Shower, W.C. and Wardrobe.
Rooms Nos. 105 and 106 contain Single Beds, Bathroom, W.C. and Wardrobe.
Rooms Nos. 109, 110, 114 and 115 contain 2 Single Beds, Bathroom and W.C.
Rooms Nos. 116, 117, 122 and 123 are Verandah Rooms containing Double Lower, Single Upper Berths, W.C. and Shower.
Rooms Nos. 118, 119, 120 and 121 contain Double Lower and Single Upper Berths, W.C. and Shower.
Rooms Nos. 103, 104, 107, 108, 111, 112, 128, 129, 134, 135, 146, 141, 146, 147, 152, 153, 158, 159, 164, 165, 170, 171, 176, 177 are Verandah Rooms containing Double Lower and Single Upper Berths.
Rooms Nos. 194 and 195 contain 2 Double Lower Berths and 2 Single Upper Berths. Other rooms contain Double Lower and Single Upper Berths.

"C" DECK
Rooms Nos. 1, 2, 3, 4 contain 2 Single Beds, Shower, Wardrobe and W.C.
Rooms Nos. 7, 8, 11 and 12 contain 2 Single Beds, Bathroom and W.C.
Rooms Nos. 14, 15, 20 and 21 are Verandah Rooms containing Double Lower, Single Upper Berth, W.C. and Shower.
Rooms Nos. 16, 17, 18, and 19 contain Double Lower and Single Upper Berths, W.C. and Shower.
Rooms Nos. 5, 6, 9, 10, 26, 27, 32, 33, 38, 39, 44, 45, 50, 51, 56, 57, 62, 63, 68, 69, 75 are Verandah Rooms containing Double Lower and Single Upper Berths.
Rooms E, F, G, H, J, K, L, M contain Twin Beds, W.C., Shower and Wardrobe.
Other Rooms contain Double Lower and Single Upper Berths.

Nearly all staterooms on decks B and C of the *Richelieu* afforded their occupants complete privacy since there were no outside passageways for most of the length of the ship on those decks. (Author's collection.)

Lake St. John

Saguenay River

JONQUIÈRE
ARVIDA
CHICOUTIMI
BAGOTVILLE

(Ha Ha Bay)

CAPE TRINITY
CAPE ETERNITY

PORTNEUF
MILLE VACHES
CAPE BON DÉSIR
GRAND BERGERONNES
TADOUSSAC

St. Lawrence River

Bi

TROIS PISTO
ILE VERTE

(Manoir Richelieu)   MURRAY BAY

CACOUNA
RIVIÈRE DU LOUP

STE. ANNE De BEAUPRÉ

QUÉBEC

CAP ROUGE

LAUZON
LÉVIS

CAP-DE-LA-MADELEINE
THREE RIVERS

The S.S. Richelieu cruise through Historical French Canada

SOREL

VERCHÈRES

VARENNES

MONTREAL

BOUCHERVILLE

MONTREAL

BOSTON

TORONTO
BUFFALO
DETROIT
CHICAGO
CLEVELAND
NEW YORK
PHILADELPHIA
WASHINGTON

From the map at the right you will see that Montreal is easily accessible from your home by rail, plane, bus or automobile.

had insufficient passenger capacity, and the propeller *Cape Eternity* had such a reputation for slowness that the second part of her name reportedly was the butt of many jokes.

At this time, only one C.S.L. steamer had actually been built for the Saguenay, and she was yet another beauty from the drawing board of the esteemed Arendt Angstrom. That ship, fittingly enough, was called the *Saguenay*. A propeller vessel 290 feet long with a single well-proportioned stack, she was constructed for the R. & O. by the eminent Fairfield shipbuilding company of Glasgow, and crossed the Atlantic from Scotland to Canada in the summer of 1911. The *Saguenay* introduced a level of comfort to her route that popularized it so much that C.S.L. had to keep adding ships to serve it.

Left: Passengers on the *Richelieu* got to see more of the St. Lawrence. Unlike her sister ships, she sailed the river east of Tadoussac, travelling as far as Bic and Portneuf before turning around. (C.S.L. brochure, author's collection.)

Three years after assigning the *Richelieu* to the Saguenay service, company directors approved the construction of another steamer for the route at C.S.L.'s own Davie Shipbuilding yard near Quebec City. To help design the new ship, which would be named *St. Lawrence*, C.S.L. reached across the

Below: The *Saguenay* was the last steamer delivered to the Richelieu and Ontario before it became part of C.S.L., and among the prettiest. (C.S.L. photo, Marine Museum of the Great Lakes.)

Above: The paddle-wheeler *Cape Diamond* operated for C.S.L. in the 1920s between Quebec, seen here, and the Saguenay. She called at smaller ports that the company's larger steamers bypassed. (C.S.L. photo, Marine Museum of the Great Lakes at Kingston.)

border to choose Herbert C. Sadler, a professor of naval architecture at the University of Michigan who had often worked with Frank E. Kirby, famed for his designs of the great Lake Erie paddle wheelers of the Detroit and Cleveland Navigation Co. and Cleveland and Buffalo Transit Co.

Sadler, working in collaboration with Alex Campbell, Davie's naval architect, came up with the plans for a 350-foot-long propeller ship that bore a fair resemblance to the *Richelieu;* both vessels had four decks and two raked funnels. The *St. Lawrence*, however, was slightly larger and arguably sleeker because she carried her lifeboats on

the hurricane deck rather than atop it as on the *Richelieu*.

Construction of the new $1.2-million steamer began in August 1926. Before the year was out, the company would order two slightly larger versions of the *St. Lawrence*, also to be designed by Sadler and Campbell and built by Davie. Regrettably, the two additional ships would be the last traditional passenger vessels with overnight accommodations built for service on the Great Lakes or St. Lawrence River.

Authorization to build the two additional ships, granted by C.S.L.'s board in late November of 1926, came just days

after the company's elegant *Montreal* was destroyed by fire. (See nearby "The Making (and Unmaking) of the *Montreal*.") One of the new ships would replace her; the other would replace the first *Quebec*, by now more than sixty years old. Like those two vessels, the new ones — which would be christened *Tadoussac* and *Quebec* — were intended primarily for the 177-mile overnight run between Montreal and Quebec but also suited for service to the Saguenay.

The clean lines of the *St. Lawrence* were all the more evident when her hull was fully exposed in a dry dock. Her hand-carved trailboard at the bow is the one on display at the Marine Museum of the Great Lakes at Kingston, Ontario. (Société historique Pierre-de-Saurel, SHPS_20100719-018.)

THE MAKING (AND UNMAKING) OF THE *MONTREAL*

Beautiful as the *Montreal* was, she had a remarkably tortuous and troubled beginning and a tragic ending.

As Jay Bascom relates in his splendid history of the ship for the Toronto Marine Historical Society, the first stage of her construction was complicated enough. Though she was launched at Toronto (in February 1902), the *Montreal* couldn't be completed there because she was 340 feet long — too big for the canals that all ships but the specially designed rapids steamers used when travelling down the St. Lawrence from Prescott to Montreal, which would be her home base. That left the R. & O. with no choice but to send its newest ship down the rapids, a challenge since even without her superstructure she drew 7 feet, 7 inches of water, more than a foot greater than the deepest draft of the company's regular rapids steamers.

Nonetheless, the *Montreal*, built up to only her main deck to minimize her draft, successfully navigated the rapids in May 1902, when the river was higher than normal, becoming what is believed to be the largest vessel ever to accomplish this feat. But it was the second stage of her construction that would prove far more harrowing.

Once out of the rapids, the steamer was taken to the R. & O.'s shipyard at Sorel, Quebec, to have her superstructure added. But as she was nearing completion there in early 1903, a fire damaged the *Montreal* so severely that the company abandoned her to the insurance underwriters. Fortunately, the story doesn't end there. After an inspection of the ship in a dry dock revealed that her hull and machinery were salvageable, the R. & O. reacquired her from the underwriters and set about rebuilding her. The *Montreal* finally entered service in 1905 — two years later than planned.

The *Montreal* was less fortunate the second time that flames engulfed her. Sailing for C.S.L. in freight-only service on the St. Lawrence in late 1926, after the passenger season had ended, she was raked by a fire of undetermined origin that left the lovely vessel a total loss and five crew members unaccounted for. It was an untimely end for what was arguably one of the most graceful steamers ever to ply the inland waters of North America.

If C.S.L. directors ended 1926 on an expansive note, they could only have been dismayed by what occurred early in the new year. Barely three weeks into it, a fire of unknown origin nearly destroyed the interior of the *St. Lawrence* while she was under construction, wiping out months of work and raising the distinct possibility that she would be unable to enter service by June 1927, as planned. Nonetheless, the ship was finished on schedule in what must have been an extraordinary feat by the Davie shipyard. (It probably didn't hurt that C.S.L. owned the shipyard.)

The *St. Lawrence* proved her worth in her first summer. W.H. Coverdale, who had succeeded Norcross as C.S.L.'s president in 1922, alluded to the new ship's contribution to passenger traffic when he informed shareholders at the company's 1928 annual meeting that the total number of passengers carried by the steamship line had increased by 75,000 in the previous year. It was the last increase reported by C.S.L for quite a few years.

Even in 1927, not everything apparently had gone well for the Montreal-Quebec City part of the route. At the end of the season,

Right: Here, the *Turbinia* is plying the St. Lawrence on her short-lived daytime service between Montreal and Quebec. (Jay Bascom.)

Below: Characteristically for the 1920s, the music room and lounge of the *St. Lawrence* reflected a trend away from the ornate interiors of earlier ships in the C.S.L. fleet. (Bibliothèque et Archives nationales du Quebec, S.J. Hayward photo, P547.S2.SS3.P813.)

MONTREAL ✦ QUEBEC
AND SAGUENAY RIVER SERVICE

CANADA STEAMSHIP LINES

C.S.L. retired the *Turbinia*, which had provided a daytime passenger service between those cities for two summers. (The handsome 1904-vintage British-built ship, the first steam-turbine vessel to be constructed for the Great Lakes, previously had proved a disappointment when operating on C.S.L.'s Toronto-Hamilton service on Lake Ontario, which also ended in 1927.)

The entry into service of the splendid *Tadoussac* and *Quebec* in 1928 presumably boosted patronage on the Montreal-Quebec City run, but not enough to increase the company's overall passenger traffic that year; it actually declined. And another steamer withdrawal occurred when the *Quebec* of

1865, which was renamed *Ste. Anne de Beaupre* after the new *Quebec* took her old run, was retired at the end of the 1928 season. With her withdrawal, the last of C.S.L.'s paddlewheelers on the Montreal-Quebec City-Saguenay route was gone.

Of the five remaining propeller ships on the route, the oldest and smallest — the *Saguenay* of 1911 — went first. Although she operated in passenger services through 1931, the *Saguenay* was dropped from C.S.L.'s timetable the following year. She did, however, carry package freight (general merchandise) later in the decade before going into long-term lay-up at Sorel, where she is said to have housed workers in local

The poster shows the second *Quebec* in her original colours sailing the St. Lawrence beneath an outsized rendering of the Citadelle military installation at Quebec. (Author's collection.)

The *Tadoussac*, with only her hull colour suggesting she will soon be eligible to join the Great White Fleet, is being fitted out in 1928 in the Champlain Dry Dock, adjacent to the Davie shipyard in Lauzon, Quebec. (Library and Archives Canada/Andrew Audubon Merrilees fonds/ PA-171041.)

Multiple flights of exterior stairs near the bow were a distinctive feature of the four steamers added to the Montreal-Saguenay route in the 1920s. C.S.L. liked this feature so much that it installed a third flight, from B deck to A deck, on the *Tadoussac*, seen here, and *Quebec* after they debuted. The *Richelieu* and *St. Lawrence* entered service without such stairs, but each got two flights later in their careers. (The Steamship Historical Society of America archives.)

defense industries during World War II. C.S.L. sold the *Saguenay* in 1946 to a shipping company in China, where she was destroyed during a typhoon five years later.

Ironically, by the early 1930s the *Tadoussac* and the *Quebec* were operating all the way to the Saguenay while the slightly smaller *St. Lawrence* and *Richelieu*, both originally intended for the longer run, were maintaining the daily Montreal-Quebec City service, for which the two newest ships had been built. In later years, all four steamers covered the entire route.

By the standards of their day, the remaining quartet of steamers seemed particularly passenger friendly. Every stateroom on these four ships was an outside room with hot and cold running water. "Each room is open to

Above: The second *Quebec* strikes a handsome pose, quite likely on her maiden voyage since she is festooned with pennants from stem to stern. (Library and Archives Canada, Hayward Studios fonds, PA-059790.)

Left: The cheery dining room of the *Quebec*, shown here early in her career, could accommodate 200 people at a single sitting. (C.S.L. photo, Marine Museum of the Great Lakes at Kingston.)

Dinner

LOBSTER COCKTAIL   MARASCHINO PINEAPPLE COCKTAIL
LOGANBERRY JUICE   TOMATO JUICE
CELERY HEARTS   GREEN OLIVES

CREAM OF MUSHROOM   CONSOMME VERMICELLI

BOILED SAGUENAY SALMON,
SHRIMP SAUCE

BAKED SPICED HAM,
SPINACH, CINNAMON PEACH

● ROAST YOUNG TURKEY,
CRANBERRY SAUCE, TINY LIMA BEANS

ROAST PRIME RIBS OF BEEF
NATURAL GRAVY

ASSORTED COLD CUTS
TURKEY, HAM, BEEF

LYONNAISE, BOILED, OR CREAMED POTATOES

FRESH VEGETABLE SALAD BOWL
HEART OF LETTUCE
MIXED FRUIT SALAD
DRESSINGS: FRENCH, ROQUEFORT. RUSSIAN OR MAYONNAISE

CHERRY PIE, CHANTILLY   CARAMEL SUNDAE
RUM PARFAIT   CHOCOLATE OR VANILLA ICE CREAM

CHEESE { OKA   CANADIAN   ROQUEFORT   OLD ENGLISH   GRUYERE   STILTON

DEMI-TASSE

Diner

COCKTAIL AU HOMARD   COCKTAIL AUX ANANAS ET CERISES
JUS DE MURES   JUS DE TOMATE
COEUR DE CELERI   OLIVES VERTES

CREME DE CHAMPIGNONS   CONSOMME VERMICELLE

SAUMON BOUILLI DU SAGUENAY,
SAUCE CREVETTE

JAMBON EPICE AU FOUR,
EPINARDS, PECHE A LA CANELLE

● DINDONNEAU ROTI,
SAUCE CANNEBERGES, FEVES DE LIMA

COTES DE BOEUF ROTIES,
SAUCE NATURE

PLAT DE VIANDES FROIDES,
SALADE DE POMMES DE TERRE, CHUTNEY

POMMES DE TERRE LYONNAISE, BOUILLIES OU A LA CREME

SALADE DE LEGUMES FRAIS
COEUR DE LAITUE
SALADE DE FRUITS
ASSAISONNEMENTS: FRANCAISE, ROQUEFORT, RUSSE OU MAYONNAISE

TARTE AUX CERISES, CHANTILLY   SUNDAE AU CARAMEL
PARFAIT AU RHUM   CREME GLACEE CHOCOLAT OU VANILLE

FROMAGE { OKA   CANADIEN   ROQUEFORT   OLD ENGLISH   GRUYERE   STILTON

DEMI-TASSE

● S.S. Tadoussac ●

Above: Menus on the Montreal-Saguenay ships initially were only in English but later were written in French as well, as in this sample from the *Tadoussac*. (Author's collection.)

Right: "A spacious, homelike bedroom" is how a C.S.L. brochure described this stateroom on an unidentified Saguenay steamer. (C.S.L. photo, Marine Museum of the Great Lakes at Kingston.)

the sunlight and the cool river breezes," noted a C.S.L. brochure, which went on to say, "Every stateroom has push-button service — more than half of them have private toilets." As for the steamers' dining rooms, "extra wide observation windows afford an unimpeded view of the passing scenic beauty with which the St. Lawrence waterway and the Saguenay River are so richly endowed."[10]

While the Depression hammered business at most of C.S.L.'s divisions, including passenger services, during much of the 1930s, World War II, when passenger traffic improved substantially, brought its own challenges. Fear of losing vessels to enemy action prompted the company in the spring of 1943 to place war-risk insurance on the four passenger ships operating east of Quebec City. (C.S.L. dropped the insurance a year later after deciding it was unnecessary.)

As it turned out, the biggest threat to the company's passenger fleet in the east-of-Quebec City service in 1943 wasn't torpedoes from German U-boats but two of its own steamers. The *Tadoussac* and the *Richelieu* collided in the St. Lawrence that August in an accident that cost the lives of two passengers on the latter vessel and took her out of service for nearly a week at the height of the season. The *Tadoussac* was held four-fifths responsible for the collision, the *Richelieu* the rest.

Although the postwar period started off well enough for C.S.L.'s passenger division, it soon went into irreversible decline as ship disasters and competition from other modes of transportation took their toll. The division's share of total corporate revenues plummeted by thirty percent between 1946 and 1949, the last year the company fielded steamers on its five traditional passenger routes. Down to just two routes in the 1950

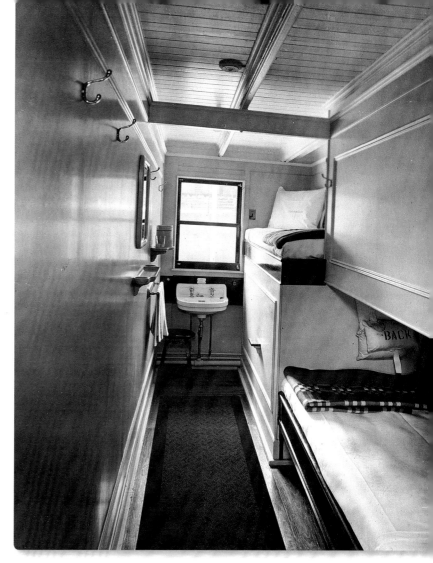

season — Toronto-Niagara and Montreal-Quebec City-Saguenay — the passenger division's share of revenues fell sharply again that year. Also contributing to the drop was the loss of the *Quebec* by fire in August 1950. (See chapter seven, "C.S.L's Trials by Fire.")

By 1952, only the Montreal-Quebec City-Saguenay service remained but its days, too, were numbered. Although earnings of the operation — which now consisted of just the *Richelieu, St. Lawrence,* and *Tadoussac* — improved for a while, they were in decline by the early 1960s. And Edgar Andrew Collard writes in *Passage to the Sea*, his history of C.S.L., that in 1965 the ships were carrying as few as fifty passengers each, when they had accommodation for nine times that number.

Every inch of space was precious in these passenger quarters. (C.S.L. photo, Marine Museum of the Great Lakes at Kingston.)

One C.S.L. passenger steamer meeting another was an occasion not to be missed. Here, in the early postwar era, an unidentified vessel on the Montreal-Saguenay service is about to pass the *Quebec.* (C.S.L. photo, Marine Museum of the Great Lakes at Kingston.)

Moreover, even though its three remaining passenger steamers had been fitted with radar in the late 1940s, the company was worried about the risk of collisions with other ships in the St. Lawrence, which had grown increasingly congested by the 1960s. C.S.L. had reason to worry: In August 1961, the *Tadoussac* (7,000 gross tons) had collided in dense fog near Quebec City with the Cunard passenger liner *Carinthia* (22,000 gross tons). While there were no casualties and damage to neither vessel was extensive, a head-on collision reportedly was averted only by desperate last-minute manoeuvres by the ships' pilots.

Against this bleak backdrop, C.S.L. announced in late 1965 that it was retiring its last passenger steamers. All three were towed to Belgium the following year for scrapping, and there the *Richelieu* and *St.*

The radar antenna atop the pilothouse of the *Richelieu* indicates that this particularly fine picture of her was taken in the postwar period. (C.S.L. photo, Marine Museum of the Great Lakes at Kingston.)

Lawrence met their demise. The *Tadoussac*, however, was resold and wound up first in Copenhagen as a floating home for Polish refugees and later as a land-bound hotel and restaurant marooned in the sands of the United Arab Emirates.

Even scrapping seems a better fate than that.

CHAPTER 6

The Outlier: C.S.L.'s Northern Exposure

Canada Steamship Lines' Northern Navigation Division was the outlier in the company's superb passenger transportation system.

The Northern's longest-surviving service — between Detroit and Duluth, Minnesota — operated in waters so far to the west that its ships didn't interconnect with the company's passenger steamers in Eastern Canada on the Niagara-to-the-Sea route. (See the map inside the front cover.) But despite its standalone status, the Northern division was a big winner for both C.S.L. and its passengers.

For the company, the Northern was a good moneymaker in large part because its three biggest and best-known ships, in their heyday, carried not only hundreds of passengers apiece but cargo in much greater quantities than C.S.L.'s passenger ships in Eastern Canada. The difference reflects the fact that the Northern was an important maritime link in one of Canada's transcontinental rail systems, more about which later.

For passengers, the Northern Navigation boats, which operated over Lakes Huron and Superior and three extremely busy rivers in the Great Lakes system, offered scenic delights, pampering aboard ship, and an escape from the often-sweltering cities of the American Midwest, where air-conditioning was not yet commonplace. Thus, C.S.L. brochures promised "ozone-laden lake breezes"[1] aboard its ships on this route and advised prospective travellers that at bedtime they would find in their staterooms "all the warm blankets you need (and you will need them, for even summer nights are bracing on the great lakes)."[2]

The seven-day, 1,600-mile Detroit-Duluth round-trip was offered from mid-June through early September, but in the spring and fall Northern Navigation steamers travelled only part of the route, plying between Sarnia, Ontario, on Lake Huron, in the east, and Port Arthur (now part of Thunder Bay) on Lake Superior, in the west. That round-trip took about half as long but still included many beauty spots.

Ship watchers most assuredly would have loved trips aboard the Northern steamers. Consider, for example, the passage through the "Soo" locks at Sault Ste. Marie on the St. Mary's River, which connects Lakes Superior and Huron. Passengers would have seen, according to a C.S.L. brochure, a waterway so heavily used that "in eight months pass three times as many vessels as pass through either the Panama or Suez Canal during the course of an entire year."[3] (The Soo locks shut down with the onset of winter and usually didn't reopen until around early April.)

If passengers boarded at Detroit or neighbouring Windsor, Ontario, across the Detroit River, they would have seen still more ships since that river reputedly was the busiest in the world in the first half of the twentieth century. As at the Soo, the mix of vessels was an eclectic one that included large passenger steamers, huge bulk carriers laden with iron ore, coal, or grain, and trim private yachts.

Some of the sights landward were equally fascinating, if not always beautiful. There was the impressive skyline of downtown Detroit, with its cluster of office towers attesting to its longtime status as the world's pre-eminent auto-making city. There was the gritty industrial landscape at Sarnia, which was, C.S.L. informed passengers, home to steel mills, foundries and — can you wait for it? — "the largest petroleum refinery of the British Empire."[4] There was also the largely unspoiled natural beauty of the wooded banks of the St. Mary's River and, on the approach to Port Arthur, Thunder Cape, at the tip of a magnificent peninsula with a distinctive rock formation, visible miles away on Lake Superior, known as the Sleeping Giant.

But land would have been out of sight for a good part of the voyage. Lake Superior, the world's largest body of fresh water, where the Northern ships spent more than a day and a half in each direction if they went as far west as Duluth, is 420 miles long and, on average, eighty miles in width. Fortunately, C.S.L. devised imaginative ways for passengers to occupy their time. Aboard the ships, there were barbershops, beauty parlours, daily tea dances, and a "mile march" (six times around the promenade deck) led by a Scottish piper, concerts every evening and even a daily newspaper, *The Northern Navigator*.

The three Northern Navigation boats offering such amenities were the 340-foot-long *Huronic* of 1901, the 365-foot *Hamonic* of 1909, and the 385-foot *Noronic* of 1913, the Northern's flagship, launched the same year as Canada Steamship Lines came into existence. (The largest of C.S.L.'s predecessor companies, Richelieu and Ontario Navigation Co., had acquired Northern Navigation two years earlier.)

To be sure, the careers of two of these ships ended prematurely — and tragically. Fire destroyed the *Hamonic* in 1945 and the *Noronic* four years later, this time with a loss of 118 lives, the deadliest disaster of its kind in Great Lakes history.

But each of the trio managed to serve C.S.L. well for more than three decades, a very respectable span. And it reflects the ships' money-making potential that while the company was winnowing its fleet of passenger steamers on the eastern Canadian runs in the late 1920s and 1930s, the trio kept running for years afterward, although in the case of the *Huronic*, in freight service only.

Above: After having discharged passengers at Detroit, seen in the background, the *Noronic* is headed across the Detroit River for Windsor, ON, where her remaining eastbound passengers will disembark. (C.S.L. photo, Marine Museum of the Great Lakes at Kingston.)

Right: Passengers on this Northern Navigation boat could even get a haircut, a rarity on Great Lakes steamers. (C.S.L. photo, Marine Museum of the Great Lakes at Kingston.)

NORTHERN NAVIGATION CO. STEAMER HURONIC.

(Bibliothèque et Archives nationales du Quebec collection Magella Bureau, P547.S2.SS3. P156.)

This view of the *Huronic* shows her with an enclosed upper pilothouse that had been installed by the early 1920s. Previously, officers used an open bridge, which exposed them to inclement weather. (Courtesy the Jay Bascom collection.)

Good taste prevailed in the interior décor of the *Hamonic* as this simply finished but cozy nook on her spar deck demonstrates. (Courtesy the Jay Bascom collection.)

The *Hamonic* was considered to be the hand-somest of the Big Three Northern steamers, and her fans can point to this exceptionally good picture of her to make their case. (Capt. W.J. Taylor photo, Jay Bascom collection.)

These three propeller-driven ships could hardly have looked more different from other passenger steamers in the C.S.L. fleet.

The Northern trio sported a no-nonsense livery of black hulls and white superstructures, whereas the boats on C.S.L.'s other passenger services were painted white from the main deck up. And, even more distinctively, each of the three Northern boats had her stack and engines placed well aft, giving the ships more unobstructed space for carrying freight; the steamers on the company's other passenger routes had engines located roughly amidships. (About the only obvious exterior feature the Northern's vessels shared with the others was a red, white, and black colour scheme

for smokestacks, which C.S.L. adopted from the Northern in the early 1920s.)

Freight was hugely important to the Northern because a few years before its vessels entered the Canada Steamship Lines fleet, it had reached an agreement with the Grand Trunk and Grand Trunk Pacific railways giving the Northern the exclusive right to transport their freight and passengers between Sarnia, Port Arthur, and Duluth. (The words "Grand Trunk Route" appeared on the ships' bows for some years afterward.)

Curiously, by late 1919, C.S.L.'s president, J.W. Norcross, was advocating the sale of Northern Navigation to the newly minted, government-owned Canadian National Railways, which had agreed to buy

both Grand Trunk railways. He reminded C.S.L.'s executive committee that while the past season had been the most profitable ever for the Northern, it had lost money in the previous few years. Should its revenue decline in future years, he warned, the Northern would fail to earn its proportion of C.S.L.'s common dividend.

As it turned out, Northern Navigation would survive as a part of C.S.L. for another thirty years. In retrospect, Norcross's pessimism seems very misguided: By 1923, when he was no longer president, the Northern was the biggest contributor toward operating net earnings of the company's four passenger divisions and second only to its bulk-cargo freighters as a source of corporate profits.

One reason for the division's fine performance was, of course, the lucrative freight side of the business. Hauling package freight westbound and flour and feed eastbound kept the *Huronic* and *Hamonic* sailing between Sarnia (or, more precisely, the adjacent village of Port Edward) and Port Arthur from early April, ice conditions permitting, to as late as December, when the Soo locks were closed for the season. The two ships would carry passengers from around early May until around early October.

The *Hamonic* is carrying large amounts of freight on this off-season trip, which explains why she's riding lower at the bow than when she carried passengers. As a precaution against damage from high seas in the off-season, her observation salon windows, at the forward end of the promenade deck, have been shuttered. (Capt. W.J. Taylor photo, Jay Bascom collection.)

The *Noronic* is seen here in June 1931 during one of her first visits to Toronto. From right, the other passenger steamers are C.S.L.'s *Cayuga*, operating on the Niagara run, and Canadian National Steamers' *Dalhousie City*, heading out the harbour for Port Dalhousie, ON. (Courtesy the Jay Bascom collection.)

The *Noronic*, although occasionally used for carrying cargo in the autumn, usually spent her time operating between Detroit and Duluth from mid-June to early September, making special cruises immediately before and after her summer season to ports not on her normal itinerary. (On some post-season cruises, she would travel to Toronto and then through the Thousand Islands to Prescott, Ontario, on the St. Lawrence, which was as far east as ships of her size could go before the opening of the St. Lawrence Seaway in 1959.)

It didn't hurt that both C.S.L. and Canadian National promoted the Northern's service as a refreshing break for those making a transcontinental rail trip; for many summers, C.N. operated special trains from Toronto to the steamer dock at Point Edward and

from Winnipeg, Manitoba, to the pier in Port Arthur. (The railroad's arch-rival, Canadian Pacific, offered similar dockside train connections to its two elegant passenger steamers which plied Lakes Huron and Superior, the *Keewatin* and the *Assiniboia*.)

The Northern operation reportedly reached its peak of popularity with passengers in the 1920s. An economic boom, the carefully conceived array of social activities offered on the three ships and the fact that alcohol, banned in Prohibition-era America, could be served on Canadian vessels all contributed to the heavy patronage of the three C.S.L. steamers in that era.

But the passenger side of the business declined enough during the Great Depression for C.S.L. to turn the *Huronic*, the oldest member of the trio, into a freight-only ship in

Right: After the *Huronic* became purely a cargo carrier, the passenger cabins that once lined her top deck were removed, leaving her looking like this. (Macaulay photo, courtesy the Jay Bascom collection.).

Below: While the heyday for the Northern division's passenger trade reportedly was in the 1920s, it wasn't always smooth sailing for the steamers themselves during that decade. Here, the *Huronic* is stranded on Lucille Island, which she plowed into during a heavy fog in Lake Superior in August 1928. (Courtesy the Jay Bascom collection.)

~Vacation trips on~
THE TIDELESS SEAS
of North America

By the Inland Liners of the

CANADA STEAMSHIP LINES
Northern Navigation Division

SPRING AND FALL SAILINGS	MIDSUMMER SAILINGS	All times shown are, EASTERN STANDARD TIME except where CENTRAL STANDARD TIME is indicated thus (CT) AM light type. PM heavy type.	MIDSUMMER SAILINGS	SPRING AND FALL SAILINGS
Thurs. May 2, 16, 30, June 13, Sept. 19 **Tues.** May 7, 21, June 4, Sept. 10, 24 **Sat.** May 11, 25, June 8, Sept. 14, 28 SS. "Hamonic"	**June 17 to September 6** See Note "A"		**June 21 to September 10** See Note "B"	**Sat.** May 4, 18, June 1, 15, Sept. 21 **Thurs.** May 9, 23, June 6, Sept. 12, 26 **Mon.** May 13, 27, June 10, Sept. 16, 30 SS. "Hamonic"
WESTBOUND—READ DOWN	WESTBOUND—READ DOWN		EASTBOUND—READ UP	EASTBOUND—READ UP
. . . .	**9:30** Fri.-Mon.	Lv. Windsor........Ont. Ar. (Gov't Dock)	**5:00** Fri.-Mon.	. . . .
. . . .	**11:00** Fri.-Mon.	Lv. Detroit........Mich. Ar. (G. T. Ry.)	**4:00** Fri.-Mon.	. . . .
. . . .	6:45 Sat.-Tue.	Ar. Sarnia........Ont. Lv. (Pt. Edward)	11:30 Fri.-Mon.	. . . .
4:00 Tue.-Sat.-Thur. 9:45 Wed.-Sun.-Fri.	**4:00** Sat.-Tue. 9:45 Sun.-Wed.	Lv. Sarnia........Ont. Ar. Ar. Sault Ste. Marie.Ont. Lv. (C. S. L. Dock)	6:30 Fri.-Mon. 10:30 Thur.-12:15 Sun.	6:30 Sat.-Wed.-Mon. 10:30 Fri.-Tue.-Sun.
12:00 Noon Wed.-Sun.-Fri.	**12:00 Noon** Sun.-Wed.	Lv. Sault Ste. Marie.Ont. Ar.	8:30 Thur.-Sun.	8:30 Fri.-Tue.-Sun.
6:30 Thur.-Mon.-Sat.	6:30 Mon.-Thur.	Ar. Port Arthur.....Ont. Lv. (C. N. R. Dock)	**1:00** Wed.-Sat.	**1:00** Thur.-Mon.-Sat.
	6:30 Mon.-Thur.	Lv. Port Arthur.....Ont. Ar. Ar. Fort William....Ont. Lv. (C. P. R. Dock)	9:30 Wed.-Sat.	
	. . . .	Lv. Fort William....Ont. Ar.	6:15 Wed.-Sat.	
	8.00 (CT) Fri.-Tue.	Ar. Duluth........Minn. Lv. (Nor. Pac. Dock No. 4)	**4:30** (CT) Fri.-Tue.	

Note "A"
Westbound-Midsummer Sailings
From Windsor and Detroit
SS. "Noronic" Fridays
SS. "Hamonic" Mondays
Sailings from **Sarnia** one day later.

Note "B"
Eastbound-Midsummer Sailings
From Duluth
SS. "Noronic" Tuesdays
SS. "Hamonic" Fridays
Sailings from **Port Arthur** one day later.

All schedules will be adhered to as closely as possible, but the Company will not hold itself responsible for detention account stress of weather or other unavoidable causes, nor for delayed connections of its own steamers or others, and reserves the right to alter any schedule with or without notice.

Time Tables of connecting lines where shown, are compiled from information available at time of going to press, but such schedules are not guaranteed and are subject to change without notice.

Account United States Coasting Laws, Detroit passengers going to Duluth or Duluth passengers going to Detroit, must board and leave ships at Windsor, Ont.

Can. Pac. Ry.	Canadian National Railways		Through rail and steamer connections between Toronto, Sarnia, Port Arthur and Winnipeg	Canadian National Railways		Can. Pac. Ry.	
Entire Season	Until June 25 and September 3 to 28	June ⊠29 to August 31		June 28 to August 30◊	Until June 24 and September 3 to 28	Until June 24	June 25 to Sept. 9
✱	8:30 Tue.-Sat.-Thur.	11:30 Sat.-Tue.	Lv. Toronto........Ont. Ar.	11:50 Fri.-Mon.	**3:25** Sat.-Wed.-Mon.	✱	✱
	9:35 Tue.-Sat.-Thur.	**12:30** Sat.-Tue.	Lv. Hamilton......Ont. Ar.	10:50 Fri.-Mon.	**2:20** Sat.-Wed.-Mon.		
	10:23 Tue.-Sat.-Thur.	**1:12** Sat.-Tue.	Lv. Brantford......Ont. Ar.	10:12 Fri.-Mon.	**1:40** Sat.-Wed.-Mon.		
	10:35 Tue.-Sat.-Thur.	**1:23** Sat.-Tue.	Lv. Paris..........Ont. Ar.	9:58 Fri.-Mon.	**1:24** Sat.-Wed.-Mon.		
	11:07 Tue.-Sat.-Thur.	**1:43** Sat.-Tue.	Lv. Woodstock.....Ont. Ar.	9:38 Fri.-Mon.	**1:01** Sat.-Wed.-Mon.		
	11:21 Tue.-Sat.-Thur.	**1:55** Sat.-Tue.	Lv. Ingersoll.......Ont. Ar.	9:27 Fri.-Mon.	**12:45** Sat.-Wed.-Mon.		
	12:00 Tue.-Sat.-Thur.	**2:20** Sat.-Tue.	Lv. London........Ont. Ar.	9:02 Fri.-Mon.	11:59 Sat.-Wed.-Mon.		
	1:15 Tue.-Sat.-Thur. Bus transfer to Steamer.	. . . . **3:45** Sat.-Tue.	Ar. Sarnia........Ont. Lv. Ar. Sarnia........Ont. Lv. (Pt. Edward)	. . . . ◊**7:35** Fri.-Mon.	10:25 Sat.-Wed.-Mon. Bus transfer to Station.		
	4:00 Tue.-Sat.-Thur.	**4:00** Sat.-Tue.	Lv. Sarnia........Ont. Ar. (Pt. Edward)	6:30 Fri.-Mon.	6:30 Sat.-Wed.-Mon.		
	12:00 Noon Wed.-Sun.-Fri. 6:30 Thur.-Mon.-Sat.	**12:00 Noon** Sun.-Wed. 6:30 Mon.-Thur.	Lv. Sault Ste. Marie.Ont. Lv. Ar. Port Arthur.....Ont. Lv.	10:30 Thur. **12:15** Sun. **1:00** Wed.-Sat.	10:30 Fri.-Tue.-Sun. **1:00** Thur.-Mon.-Sun.		
✱ 8:15 **7:50** (CT)		6:30 (CT) Mon.-Thur. **7:50** (CT) Mon.-Thur.	Lv. Port Arthur.....Ont. Ar. Ar. Winnipeg......Man. Lv.	11:25 (CT) Wed.-Sat. 10:30 (CT) Tue.-Fri.		✱ 7:00 **6:45** (CT)	✱ 7:20 **7:05** (CT)

⊠June 18th, 22nd and 25th leave Toronto 8:30 a.m. arrive Sarnia 1:10 p.m.   ◊Monday Sept. 2nd leave Sarnia 10:25 a.m. arrive Toronto 3:25 p.m.
✱Schedule between Toronto and Port Arthur same as shown under Canadian National Railways.

Northern Pacific	Great Northern	Soo. Line	Northern Pacific	Great Northern	Railway Connections Between Duluth, St. Paul and Minneapolis	Northern Pacific	Great Northern	Soo. Line	Great Northern	Northern Pacific
11:30 (CT)	**4:30** (CT)	**1:00** (CT)	8:30 (CT)	8:00 (CT)	Lv. Duluth........Minn. Ar.	**12:25** (CT)	**1:50** (CT)	**6:10** (CT)	8:00 (CT)	6:30 (CT)
5:55 (CT)	**8:00** (CT)	**5:19** (CT)	**12:30** (CT)	**12:40** (CT)	Ar. St. Paul......Minn. Lv.	8:25 (CT)	9:00 (CT)	**1:50** (CT)	**4:30** (CT)	11:59 (CT)
6:40 (CT)	**7:30** (CT)	**5:50** (CT)	**2:30** (CT)	**12:10** (CT)	Ar. Minneapolis...Minn. Lv.	7:20 (CT)	9:35 (CT)	**1:15** (CT)	**5:00** (CT)	11:20 (CT)

To and from Detroit and Windsor convenient connections are available by rail and steamer.

Above: (Author's collection.)

Left: It's a measure of the importance C.S.L. attached to the *Hamonic* and *Noronic* that in the Depression year of 1934, no less, the company produced this lavish twenty-page brochure to promote them. This is the brochure's cover. (Author's collection.)

These servers waited on the *Noronic's* passengers. (C.S.L. photo, Marine Museum of the Great Lakes at Kingston.)

1934, leaving just the *Hamonic* to carry passengers between Sarnia and Port Arthur in the spring and early fall. She would join the *Noronic* on the longer Detroit-Duluth run when service resumed on that route each summer. The two steamers would follow that routine annually until the *Hamonic* was destroyed by fire in the summer of 1945.

The loss of the beautiful ship — the handsomest of the trio — failed to dampen the enthusiasm of C.S.L.'s president, W.H. Coverdale, for the Northern Navigation Division, now reduced to just two ships, only one of them, the *Noronic,* still in passenger service.

Even the year before the *Hamonic's* demise, he had announced the company's intention to build a passenger vessel for its upper lakes service "at the earliest possible time."[5] And at the annual meeting in 1946, shareholders learned that plans to replace the *Hamonic* were close to completion, and that construction would commence as soon as materials were available. As late as 1948, with the replacement still undelivered, a C.S.L. brochure mentioned a planned "new sister-ship" for the *Noronic.*[6]

By then the *Noronic* was thirty-five years old. Yet the largest propeller passenger steamer on the Great Lakes still had a lot to offer her customers as these excerpts from a company booklet, published near the end of World War II, suggest:

"Let's go aboard and look around the Noronic ... Look at her — isn't she a

beauty! Almost 400 feet long — longer than many an ocean liner — with no less than six decks [there were actually five], offering accommodations for as many as 562 passengers…. And here's a delightful surprise — the Dining Salon is *on a top deck* instead of being far down below, as in most ocean liners, and its huge observation windows give you a thrilling and unobstructed view as you sit at table.

"Another delightful gathering place is the Observation Salon, with its big wide windows and upholstered chairs. Nearby are other comfortable salons, the music room, the writing room, the smoking room, the buffet bar…"[7]

If the *Noronic* was beautiful on the inside, she was anything but on the out-

side, in the view of ship buffs. During her construction, she was given one more deck than originally intended, which made her not only homely but apparently top-heavy. In her book *Great Lakes Saga*, Anna G. Young recalls that in the *Noronic's* first season of operation, 1914, she listed over so far while being refueled at Point Edward that the steamer snapped some of her mooring lines and came to rest against the dock where she was berthed.

To improve the stability of the *Noronic,* she was sent to an American dry dock, which added six feet to her beam. The result was an odd outward flare, or bustle, in her hull near the waterline that greatly detracted from her appearance.

With long rows of windows running down both sides of the room, the *Noronic's* observation salon was aptly named. (C.S.L. photo, Marine Museum of the Great Lakes at Kingston.)

The naval architect responsible for the *Noronic* was one Lars Eric Tornroos, who, like Arendt Angstrom, was a native of Sweden and is said to have assisted him in designing the lovely *Kingston* and *Cayuga* when both men worked at the Bertram Engine Works in Toronto in the early 1900s. Tornroos's design for the *Noronic* was considerably less successful aesthetically than the one that others developed for the *Hamonic*, which, with fewer decks and a more discernible sheer (for-to-aft curvature of the hull), had much more graceful lines. (That could reflect the fact that the Frank E. Kirby of Detroit — the naval architect for so many wonderful Great Lakes passenger ships — consulted on the plans for the *Hamonic*.)

Tornroos, who served for many years as naval architect at Port Arthur Shipyard, lived for another eight years after the *Noronic*

burned at her dock in Toronto Harbour in September 1949. (See chapter seven, "C.S.L.'s Trials by Fire.") The disaster not only destroyed the Northern Navigation's flagship but also doomed some other fine, long-serving C.S.L. vessels.

As previously noted, the fire that consumed the *Noronic* led to more stringent safety regulations for Canadian passenger steamers that at C.S.L. helped to bring a quick end to service on two company routes — Toronto-Prescott, served by the *Kingston*, and Prescott-Montreal, served by the *Rapids Prince*. Even the *Huronic*, a freight-only vessel for the last fifteen years but one with a wooden superstructure, also was withdrawn at the end of the 1949 season and scrapped the next year. And there would be no "new sister-ship" for the now-destroyed *Noronic*.

Time had run out for the corporate outlier.

The six feet added to the *Noronic's* beam near her waterline subtracted from her looks, as this pre-war picture of her at Port Arthur illustrates. (Courtesy the Jay Bascom collection.)

Over the
deep

Could this be the planned (but never built) new sister ship for the *Noronic* on the cover of C.S.L.'s 1948 brochure for the Detroit-Duluth service? With her raked prow and smokestack far forward, the anonymous vessel, depicted in the "Soo" locks, looks quite modern by postwar standards and nothing like the *Noronic*. It's fun to contemplate what the artist's intent was, but we'll likely never know. (C.S.L. brochure, author's collection.)

CANADA STEAMSHIP LINES

OTHER NORTHERN NAVIGATION BOATS

While the Northern Navigation's "Big Three" were the mainstay of its operation, its fleet under Canada Steamship Lines ownership at times included several intriguing smaller passenger vessels.

Besides the aforementioned *Huronic, Hamonic,* and *Noronic* on the lucrative route across Lakes Huron and Superior, the Northern operated a number of interesting but less prominent steamers, some of which were holdovers from when it was an independent company, while others were ships that Canada Steamship dispatched to the Northern after it entered the C.S.L. fold in 1913.

Among the smaller ships that the Northern brought to C.S.L. were the *Germanic* of 1899, which operated across Georgian Bay (the eastern arm of Lake Huron) between the Ontario ports of Collingwood and Sault Ste. Marie, and the *Waubic* of 1909, which was often found on the exquisite daytime run through that bay's Thirty Thousand Islands, between Penetanguishene and Parry Sound.

For its part, C.S.L. contributed to the Northern operation at least three vessels from elsewhere in its passenger-ship empire. Two were employed during part of the 1920s in day-excursion service between Detroit and the nearby Canadian ports of Chatham and Wallaceburg, a trip that took passengers across Lake St. Clair (between Michigan and Ontario) and into the Thames and North Sydenham Rivers, respectively. Those steamers were the *Rapids King* of 1907, which had been built for the Prescott-Montreal rapids trip, and the *Thousand Islander* of 1912, which had been built for work in the upper St. Lawrence River.

In addition, C.S.L. in the 1920s transferred to Northern Navigation the *Louis Philippe,* a passenger and car ferry built for the company in 1914 for service across the St. Lawrence between Montreal and Longueil, Quebec. She operated in the same capacity for the Northern for a short time, plying the St. Clair River between Sarnia, Ontario, and Port Huron, Michigan.

Although the *Huronic, Hamonic,* and *Noronic* had long careers under the Canada Steamship Lines flag, the other vessels remained in C.S.L.'s Northern Navigation fleet for much shorter durations.

The *Germanic* was destroyed by fire in 1917, while the *Waubic* was sold by C.S.L. in 1921 for service in the St. Lawrence among the Thousand Islands, marking an end to regularly scheduled service by the Northern on Georgian Bay. The *Rapids King,* which proved unsuitable for the service out of Detroit, rejoined the Prescott-Montreal service in 1929 after extensive rebuilding. The *Thousand Islander,* the victim of ever-stiffer competition from automobiles, was sold in 1928 to another company, only to founder in a storm that fall.

Finally, the ferry *Louis Philippe* returned to its earlier route between Montreal and Longueuil but became redundant after the Montreal Harbour Bridge (now the Jacques Cartier Bridge) opened in 1930. Shortly afterward, C.S.L. sold her to a company that operated her on the St. Lawrence between Prescott, Ontario, and Ogdensburg, New York, for two decades. She was then scrapped.

CHAPTER 7

C.S.L.'s Trials by Fire

It has to be the saddest chapter in Canada Steamship Lines' long history. Within the space of just five years, the company lost three of its best passenger steamers to fire — a record almost unparalleled in modern times.

First came the *Hamonic* of C.S.L.'s Northern Navigation Division, which went up in flames in July 1945. Next came the division's flagship, the *Noronic*, whose demise, in September 1949, was accompanied by the largest loss of life of any shipboard fire on the Great Lakes. Then came the *Quebec* on C.S.L.'s Montreal-Saguenay route, which was destroyed in August 1950. In each case, hundreds of passengers were aboard the vessels when they caught fire.

The captains of the *Hamonic* and *Quebec* were authentic heroes, credited with preventing potentially large losses of life aboard their respective vessels as they were engulfed in flames. On the other hand, the master of the *Noronic* was faulted by an investigatory commission for acting as "an ordinary sailor"[1] instead of taking general charge of the ship's response to the fire as the senior officer is supposed to do. And C.S.L. itself also came in for blame.

The *Hamonic,* with 247 passengers reportedly aboard, was docked at Point Edward, Ontario, when a malfunctioning forklift truck in an adjacent warehouse caught fire. It quickly spread to a nearby shed filled with flour dust and then to the ship. The captain, Horace Beaton, recognizing that it would be impossible to disembark those aboard the ship at the now-blazing wharf, responded by backing his vessel into the St. Clair River so fast that she tore her mooring lines and gangplanks loose from the pier.

Then, so as to land the passengers and crew before fire totally consumed the ship, Beaton sent the boat full speed ahead into a nearby coal dock, intentionally grounding her. Everyone was able to leave the *Hamonic* safely, including the captain, the last one off, who reportedly was badly burned while beaching the vessel. (He went on to skipper C.S.L. ships for another twenty-two years.)

On the night that tragedy struck the *Noronic,* she also was docked — in her case at Toronto — and filled nearly to capacity. Almost all of the 524 passengers aboard were on a one-week post-season cruise that originated in Detroit and would have taken them through the Thousand Islands of the St. Lawrence River before returning to the Motor City. The ship had tied up in Toronto at 7 p.m. local time and was scheduled to depart about twenty-four hours later. In the meantime, the ship would act as a floating hotel for her passengers.

Fire destroyed the *Hamonic* at Point Edward, ON, on July 17, 1945. (Courtesy the Jay Bascom Collection.)

The fire aboard the *Noronic* was discovered shortly after 2:30 a.m. by a passenger who noticed smoke seeping from one of the ship's linen lockers. Finding it locked, he notified a crew member, and together they opened it and saw flames rising from the linen. When a fire extinguisher proved incapable of extinguishing the blaze, they grabbed a hose, only to find that no water came out. Only then, precious minutes after the discovery of the fire, did the crewman turn in the fire alarm and seek help — a delay that the head of the government inquiry, the Hon. Justice R.L. Kellock of the Supreme Court of Canada, called "fatal" in his scathing report on the disaster.[2]

He concluded that enough time was lost in the initial attempt to fight the fire that when the alarm was given, "it was no longer, in my opinion, a question of extinguishing the fire but of getting those onboard off the ship." [3]

One hundred and eighteen passengers — more than one in every five on the cruise — perished in the fire. Many, probably most, passengers were asleep when it broke out. Those who did awaken and tried to flee the ship had to battle thick smoke and flames. Some of those unable to leave the vessel on the sole gangway for passengers reached safety by jumping to the pier, although a much greater number chose to dive into the harbour from the five-deck-high ship. Although most who opted for diving survived, a few drowned.

Fire destroyed the *Noronic* at Toronto on Sept. 17, 1949. (Courtesy the Jay Bascom Collection.)

Making the tragedy all the more painful to bear was the fact that not one of the *Noronic's* 171 crewmembers died. On the night of the fire, only a skeletal crew of 15 was required to be on the ship; all the rest were free to go ashore, although how many did so is unknown.

Among those who had gone ashore was the captain, sixty-five-year-old William Taylor, a C.S.L. veteran who had skippered the *Noronic* for the previous seven years. He had returned to the ship with a female passenger about five minutes before the fire was discovered, escorted her to her stateroom, and then retired to his quarters, where a wheelsman informed him of the inferno raging two decks below. Taylor, rather than taking command of the situation, acted as if he were just another crewman and apparently came up short even in that capacity.

For instance, he acknowledged to the Kellock commission that rousing passengers and getting them off the ship was imperative once he realized the fire was too far advanced for the crew to extinguish it. "But yet," one of his interrogators asked Taylor, "you walked back from the forward end of the ship right back to the stern without seeing that a single passenger was aroused?"[4]

"I do not recall rapping on the [stateroom] windows on the way back," the *Noronic's* master replied.[5]

Was Taylor intoxicated at the time of the fire? The inquiry's findings were inconclusive. The captain himself testified that he had consumed only one drink while ashore. Two policemen who encountered him when he descended to the dock from the blazing ship said they could smell liquor on his breath but that his behaviour wasn't indicative of heavy drinking. And neither the female passenger accompanying Taylor on his shore excursion nor the taxi driver who took them back to the ship observed him to be intoxicated.

Kellock's report blamed the lack of preparedness for fire aboard the *Noronic* on the "complete complacency" that "had descended upon both the ship's officers and the management."[6] After listing the causes for the heavy loss of life and the loss of the *Noronic* herself (See nearby "A Most Damning Report"), Kellock ordered that Taylor's master's certificate be suspended for a year and that C.S.L. pay the cost of the investigation. (Taylor never shipped out again.)

The justice's report was unable, however, to determine the cause of the fire itself; the inquiry found no evidence that the fire was deliberately set, although C.S.L's lawyers believed that arson was the probable cause. They suggested that the company offer a reward for information leading to the apprehension and conviction of anyone found guilty. C.S.L.'s directors vetoed the proposal, but likely came to regret that.

Their rationale for opposing a reward, as recorded at a November 1949 board meeting, was "that it would probably work to the disadvantage of the company to give any further publicity to the fire."[7] In light of what happened the following summer, the directors' priorities at that meeting seem tragically twisted.

C.S.L's *Quebec*, with 426 passengers aboard, was steaming down the St. Lawrence en route to Tadoussac when fire broke out in one of the ship's linen lockers, the same point of origin, of course, as with the fire on the *Noronic*. As on that vessel, the fire on the *Quebec* quickly got out of control. Seven of her passengers lost their lives in a blaze that a commission headed by the Hon. Justice Fernand Choquette of the Quebec Superior Court found had been set by "the criminal hand."[8]

At the inquiry, in testimony that also had relevance for the fire on the *Noronic*, expert witnesses testified about the difficulty of starting a linen fire of life-threatening intensity without the addition of an accelerant. But the critical piece of evidence pointing to arson on the *Quebec* was the fact that her fire alarm system, in good working order when checked not long before the she burned, had been disabled at the time of the disaster.

No one was ever prosecuted but, intriguingly, Edgar Andrew Collard in his deeply researched history of C.S.L., *Passage to the Sea*, writes, "The close parallels between the two fires suggested that both had been the work of an arsonist, probably the same person."[9]

The loss of life on the *Quebec* could have been much greater were it not for the quick thinking and superb seamanship of her master, Cyril Burch. With fire engulfing his ship, he was faced with the decision of whether to spend valuable time launching lifeboats into the St. Lawrence before abandoning ship or sail her the remaining four miles to the wharf at Tadoussac, knowing that doing so only would fan the flames further. He chose the latter option. Although docking at the pier is notoriously difficult because of tricky tidal conditions, Burch was able to land there smoothly and disembark passengers. C.S.L.'s directors later gave him a $5,000 reward in appreciation for his efforts. (As for the *Quebec*, she burned at the dock during the night, right down to her main deck.)

After the *Quebec* fire, C.S.L. would remain in the passenger business for another fifteen years. Thankfully, they brought no more trials by fire.

A MOST DAMNING REPORT

"I have spoken to various officers on the ill-fated vessel, as well as to many members of the crew, and I have ascertained beyond any reasonable doubt that the tragedy was the result of one of those impenetrable blows by fate, and that there was no negligence on the part of either the officers, the crew or the company."
— Excerpt from a statement by Colonel K.R. Marshall, president of Canada Steamship Lines, issued on September 17, 1949, the day the *Noronic* was destroyed by fire.[10]

If there was ever any doubt that the *Noronic* was merely an undeserving victim of fate, the government inquiry into the tragedy surely dispelled it.

The fire that swept the thirty-six-year-old vessel "found the ship totally unprepared to deal with the situation," concluded Justice R.L. Kellock, who headed the inquiry.[11]

While the Kellock commission was unable to determine the cause of the fire, the panel placed blame for the heavy loss of life and the loss of the ship squarely on C.S.L. and her captain, William Taylor. The investigators found that the owners and the master:

- Failed to establish a continuous patrol of the ship for detecting the presence of fire. Although a card placed in staterooms assured passengers that their steamer was "patrolled day and night by experienced watchmen,"[12] the inquiry found that patrols on the *Noronic* were limited to approximately fifteen minutes out of every hour and that watchmen took the shortest possible routes, often avoiding corridors like the one with the linen locker where the fire originated.
- Failed to have any organization in place for when the ship was docked and with passengers aboard — the *Noronic*'s situation in Toronto — by which information on the outbreak of fire could have been promptly conveyed to crew members so that they could respond to the emergency.
- Failed to contemplate in any real sense the possibility of fire occurring at a dock while maintaining only fifteen crewmembers on duty.
- Failed to have any plan for arousing and getting the passengers off the ship in the event of fire while the ship was docked.
- Failed to train the crew in firefighting beyond teaching them how to operate fire extinguishers and hoses.

The report also addressed the vexing matter of why none of the *Noronic*'s 171 crew members perished in the fire. Here's the investigators' explanation: the officers who occupied the forward end of the top deck were roused by the alarm bell, which rang simultaneously in the engine room. Other crew members had their quarters at either end of the ship, at a distance from where the fire started. "They all appear to have been warned by some of their fellows and, once roused, as they were more familiar with the ship, they could, the more easily, find their way out," wrote Kellock.[13]

If only the passengers had been so fortunate!

Epilogue

The gangway, the lobby, the row of stiff chairs, each with its polished brass spittoon, the brass-edged stairway with its ornately carved banisters, the carpets with an 'R&O' design inherited from Canada Steamship Lines' predecessor the Richelieu and Ontario Navigation Company, the gingerbread woodwork, the narrow cabins, the upper bunk where you could see out the window — no wonder a little boy got little sleep, and came to wait for and love the incidents of the night.
— Lewis Evans recalling trips aboard C.S.L.'s *Montreal* and its first *Quebec* between their namesake cities in his memoir *Tides of Tadoussac: The Golden Age of a St. Lawrence Resort.*[1]

While the perils of steamer travel — all too powerfully illustrated by the *Noronic's* tragic ending — are an integral part of the Great White Fleet story, it's the pleasures of steamer travel that are the overarching theme of this book and one that I hope delights you as much as it does me.

Browsing through books and brochures about Canada Steamship Line's veritable passenger-ship empire has enabled me to revisit the reasons why this mode of travel — and this company in particular — meant so much to me and perhaps to many others as well. Let's take the mode of travel first.

Except on the C.S.L.'s Northern Navigation Division's service across Lakes Huron and Superior, both vast bodies of water, there was an intimate relationship between passenger and landscape on the company's routes. Steamer travel as practised by C.S.L. took passengers within wonderfully close range of the scenic banks of the lower Niagara River, the exquisite

Thousand Islands, the ever-present Laurentian Mountains lining the north shore of the lower St. Lawrence River, and, finally, the two "Higher than Gibraltar" capes of the awe-inspiring Saguenay River. It was a lovely way to literally get the lay of the land.

Then there were the steamers themselves. I never cease to admire the exceptionally graceful lines of the passenger ships that C.S.L. inherited from the Richelieu and Ontario Navigation Co. In particular, the *Cayuga*, the *Toronto*, the *Kingston*, the

Steamers often sailed delightfully close to land. Here, a C.S.L. ship passes the 25-foot-high statue of the Virgin Mary on Cape Trinity. As they approached the statue at night, steamers would spotlight it, reportedly moving some travellers to tears. ("Bateau Blanc au cap Trinité," Madeleine Craig donation, Musée de Charlevoix.)

Rapids Prince, the *Montreal*, and the *Saguenay* set a very high standard for naval architecture. And for that, credit goes to Arendt Angstrom, designer of them all. Thank you, Arendt Angstrom!

But the charm of these steamers went well beyond their exterior beauty. Recall, for instance, those comfy upholstered wicker armchairs provided for passengers to view the rapids of the St. Lawrence from inside the observation lounges of the *Rapids Prince* and *Rapids King* after their 1929 reconstruction. Or think of how, on the boats such as the *Tadoussac*

and the second *Quebec*, an "observation dining room" with extra wide windows was thoughtfully placed at the aft end of their main decks so that patrons could watch passing river traffic and superb scenery as they consumed their meals.

And after dinner, a 1931 C.S.L. brochure tells us, those ships offered "a high-class orchestra with a full concert and dance program every evening" and a buffet bar serving light wines and beer. How could you go wrong?[2]

Years after C.S.L. retired all its passenger boats those who once travelled aboard

Two of the naval architect Arendt Angstrom's finest achievements, the *Cayuga* (left) and the *Kingston*, often would leave Toronto Harbour together before going their separate ways, as they shortly will here. (Courtesy the Jay Bascom collection.)

them could describe the experience in such rich detail that even those who never shared it can nonetheless savour it. Here's what Lewis Evans, who rode for decades on the company's steamers between Montreal and Tadoussac, writes about "the incidents of the night" during trips he made as a child:

"The buoys dancing past like little red and black soldiers with their hands on their hips; the stop at Sorel, where always men seemed engaged in dropping iron pipes on other iron pipes; the swishing nothingness of Lake St. Peter [an especially broad part of the St. Lawrence downriver from Sorel]; and, best of all, passing the upward-bound steamer, which swooped past in a blaze of light and flurry of foam, and always an exchange of shouts from freight deck to freight deck."[3]

The child that has remained inside me for more than seven decades is still awestruck by the company that made possible the pleasures experienced by Lewis Evans and millions of other passengers. So mighty was Canada Steamship Lines that its president, W.H. Coverdale, could boast in 1928: "We have the best passenger and freight ships on the Canadian Great Lakes, and we have the most of them also, as you can prove for yourself by watching the red, white and black smokestacks either en route or in any Canadian harbor from Port Arthur and Fort William to Quebec."[4]

The sun set nearly a half-century ago over C.S.L.'s passenger ship empire, but affection for it lives on. As I can attest.

SONG BOOK

CANADA STEAMSHIP LINES

More ships on the Great Lakes and St. Lawrence bore C.S.L.'s instantly recognizable smokestack colours than any other. Even the songbooks distributed to passengers for sing-alongs featured the iconic two-stack logo that referenced the Great White Fleet. (Author's collection.)

The Peaks and Valleys of C.S.L.'s Passenger Business

The handwriting had been on the wall for decades when Canada Steamship Lines announced its withdrawal from the passenger-ship business nearly a half century ago.

The love affair with Great Lakes passenger steamers began to fade, when, as David Lancashire wrote in the *Globe and Mail*, "the first automobile sputtered down the first paved highway in Ontario, between Toronto and Hamilton in 1912." Within little more than a decade, the changes in C.S.L.'s fortunes on the passenger side of its business would be profound.[1]

As the 1920s opened, the company was carrying passengers not only on the five major routes covered in this book but also on secondary services across Lake Ontario between Toronto and Grimsby, Ontario, and Toronto and Hamilton. Those two services soon disappeared, the Grimsby one first and then Toronto-Hamilton after the end of the 1927 season. And stiffening competition from automobile travel reportedly was why C.S.L. withdrew the *Thousand Islander* from its excursion service out of Detroit in 1928, in August no less, typically the height of the vacation season.

There was more retrenchment: On the Toronto-Bay of Quinte-Prescott route, the *Cape Trinity* also was retired in 1928; the next year it was the *Corona's* turn on the Toronto-Niagara run.

After C.S.L. withdrew the *Corona* from service, she was laid up at Toronto, where her appearance had deteriorated markedly by the time this picture was taken in the 1930s. (Courtesy the Jay Bascom collection.)

Altogether, the number of passengers carried by C.S.L. steamers fell by more than a third during the 1920s, a time of great expansion for the economy in general. Although the introduction of the brand-new *St. Lawrence* to the Montreal-Quebec City-Saguenay route in 1927 helped to modestly reverse the decline, it resumed the following year despite the debuts on the Montreal-Quebec City service of the big and beautiful *Tadoussac* and *Quebec*. And this was before the beginning of the Great Depression!

After the close of the 1930 season, the first summer of the Depression, C.S.L.'s general manager, T.R. Enderby, stated that the company's passenger traffic "has suffered severely; people whose profits, paper or otherwise, have dissolved into thin air are not inclined to travel...."[2] As if to prove his point, the number of passengers carried, which had surpassed 2,000,000 in 1920, totalled just 514,000 in 1931 — a drop of nearly seventy-five percent.

1. PERCENTAGE OF TOTAL C.S.L. REVENUES FROM PASSENGER SHIPS

Year	Percentage
1924	41
1945	23
1946	26
1947	23
1948	20
1949	18
1950	10

Sources: 1924 percentage from directors meeting minutes of Dec. 9, 1924; other percentages are from company annual reports. Data for other years were unavailable to the author.

While I was unable to unearth traffic statistics for any years after 1931, C.S.L annual reports speak in general terms of improvement on the passenger side of the business by the mid-1930s. It deteriorated toward the end of the decade, however, with a smaller contribution to corporate earnings in 1938 and disappointing results again in 1939, when Canada entered World War II. That year, "passenger business disappeared in Eastern Canada," according to a somewhat hyperbolic passage in the minutes of the 1940 annual meeting; traffic held up better on the Northern Navigation Division's *Hamonic* and the *Noronic* on the upper Great Lakes. But better times lay just ahead for the entire passenger fleet.[3]

The advent of hostilities presented C.S.L. with ample opportunities to revive its passenger trade. Thus, the company's annual report for 1941 reminds readers that "'Take a Boat Trip' becomes not only a slogan for our services but a slogan which says, 'Save Gasoline!' 'Save Tires and Oil' 'Save Money' 'Return Refreshed to Your Wartime Job.'"[4]

Canadians (and undoubtedly many Americans) apparently took the message to heart. Calling 1941 "the best year in the history of the company," Coverdale told shareholders at C.S.L.'s annual meeting the following April, "It is also a pleasure to state that each and every service of the company during 1941 — with the exception of the hotels, where the loss was negligible — showed not only substantial earnings but great improvement over the previous year."[5]

Given such impressive results, it's perhaps understandable why Coverdale would tell shareholders in early 1945 — after three more years of war-induced prosperity for the company — that "there is plenty of business in sight, both passenger and freight." Or why he would press for construction of two new passenger steamers, one for the Northern Navigation Division and one for Lake Ontario.[6]

For a brief time in the postwar period, Coverdale's optimism seemed justified. Revenues from the passenger side as a proportion of the company total actually increased, rising from twenty-three percent in 1945 to twenty-six percent in 1946. That gain was especially impressive considering that C.S.L. had one less passenger ship in 1946 because of the destruction of the *Hamonic* by fire the previous summer.

But the very next year the passenger share of revenues began to slide without interruption, hitting ten percent by 1950, the last year for which I was able to find data. By the end of that summer, C.S.L. was operating four fewer steamers than it had as recently as the start of the 1949 season. Those steamers were the *Noronic* and the *Quebec*, both lost to fire, and the *Kingston* and the *Rapids Prince*, whose retirements stemmed from the prohibitive cost of modifying the forty-eight-year-old *Kingston* (which fed passengers to the *Rapids Prince*) to comply with more stringent safety regulations established in the wake of the *Noronic* disaster.

The *Kingston*, though minus her lifeboats, still looks good even as she's being towed to the scrapyard in 1950. (Courtesy the Jay Bascom collection.)

2. NUMBER OF PASSENGERS CARRIED

Year	Number of Passengers
1920	2,032,771
1926	1,442,000
1927	1,517,000
1928	1,328,000
1929	1,308,000
1931	514,000

Sources: 1920 number from C.S.L. brochure illustrated on p. 97. *Passage to the Sea: The Story of Canada Steamship Lines*, by Edgar Andrew Collard (Doubleday Canada, 1991). Data for 1926 through 1929 from reports of annual shareholder meetings in 1927, 1928, 1929, and 1930. The number of 1931 is from the company's annual report for that year, published in 1932. Data for other years were unavailable to the author.

The seaplane flying over the *Toronto* as she moved through the Thousand Islands was a harbinger of the competition from alternative modes of transportation that would ultimately doom the Great White Fleet. (Courtesy the Jay Bascom collection.)

"The increase in automobile travel is cutting deeply into passenger trades and it was believed unwise to rebuild the ancient *Kingston*," explained Col. K.R. Marshall, Coverdale's successor as president of C.S.L, in early 1950.[7]

Competition from the automobile on C.S.L.'s Montreal-Quebec-City-Saguenay passenger service took somewhat longer to be felt. Benny Beattie, who rode the company's steamers on that route for two decades beginning in the late 1930s, writes in *Tadoussac: The Sands of Summer* that the journey from Montreal to Tadoussac used to be "a long, slow drive along dusty, winding country roads. What now takes a car five hours, took two days back then."[8]

Roads were difficult and expensive to build along the rugged north shore of the St. Lawrence River to points like Tadoussac, Beattie wrote when I asked him to amplify. "Not until the 1950s," he said,

"did roads begin to improve and automobile travel begin to grow in popularity in that area."[9]

Sure enough, the increased car usage helped doom C.S.L.'s last remaining passenger route. As noted earlier, the company blamed "the inroads of automobile and air traffic" for the decline in patronage that prompted it to end the Montreal-Saguenay service in 1965. History had repeated itself.[10]

3. NUMBER OF C.S.L. PASSENGER SHIPS (SELECTED YEARS)

Year	Passenger Ships
1913–1914	51
1921	31
1927	23
1928	25
1929	22
1930	21
1935	17
1937	16
1938	12
1946	11
1949	9
1950	5
1951	4
1952–1965	3
1966	0

Notes: 1913–1914 number represents passenger and passenger/freight vessels at C.S.L.'s creation based on fleet list in "Passage to the Sea" starting on page 417. Data for 1921 through 1950, based on directors meeting minutes and annual reports, represent steamers in fleet at the start of the respective season and include passenger ships in long-term lay-up. Data for subsequent years, based on personal knowledge, represent only steamers in active service.

THE SLIPPERY SLOPE

The situation was rich with irony. Although Canada Steamship Lines attributed the withering of its passenger business partly to inroads made by auto travel, the company decades earlier had actually promoted car trips, albeit in conjunction with its steamers.

Way back in 1917, a C.S.L. magazine called *By-Water* carried an ad on its back cover trumpeting "The Newest Thing in Holidays! Try the Auto-Steamship Vacation." The ad continues: "By combining the advantages of your own automobile with the luxury of the steamers of Canada Steamship Lines, Limited, you can tap a new source of recreation."[11]

The next month's issue followed up with the enthusiastic account of a traveller who drove the 184 miles between Montreal and Quebec in nine hours, "having taken photographs on the way, and stopped for an hour and a half at Three Rivers [Trois-Rivières] for lunch." The return trip, by steamer, seemed almost an anticlimax.[12]

By the mid-1930s, you could find full-page ads for C.S.L.'s Manoir Richelieu hotel on the St. Lawrence River headlined "Just Overnight from Montreal by Palatial Steamer or Modern Highway" and urging prospective customers to "come down river from Montreal by car, or in glistening white steamer."[13]

And with the steady increase in auto travel, C.S.L. brochures by the mid-1930s no longer included maps showing the dense web of rail lines in Canada and the United States that passengers could use to reach the company's ships; prospective travellers had to undertake their own research.

You can't blame C.S.L. for adopting an "if you can't lick 'em, join 'em" approach with an up-and-coming rival mode of transportation. It was a force too great to resist. But in the end, it was C.S.L. — or, more precisely, its passenger business — that got licked.

The MANOIR Richelieu
MURRAY BAY — CANADA

SADDLE HORSES · · · SWIMMING · · · GOLF · · ·

TENNIS · · ARCHERY · · THRILLS en route · ·

A GLAMOROUS OLD-WORLD COUNTRYSIDE ·

Just Overnight from Montreal by Palatial Steamer or Modern Highway

Fortunate are they who have discovered the MANOIR RICHELIEU at Murray Bay. Here they really *live*, restfully and completely, with every conceivable facility constantly at their command. Come down river from Montreal by car, or in glistening white steamer, most modern of the world's rivercraft. Your favourite summertime sports await you in ideal surroundings; quaint Habitant villages, naiveté of a simple people, the *chansons* of Normandy, Old France in New World setting.

Rates that are Practical

You can live luxuriously yet economically as low as $9 a day, including room and meals. Return fare by boat, Montreal to Murray Bay, including meals and berth, $27.35. Take your car with you on the boat at small added cost. For full information, reservations, consult Canada Steamship Lines offices in principal cities or your travel agent.

Quebec

Three Rivers

Montreal

THE ST. LAWRENCE

RIVER

A DIVISION OF CANADA STEAMSHIP LINE

Left: By 1935, when this ad for the Manoir Richelieu appeared, C.S.L. didn't seem to care how guests reached the hotel — just as long as they reached it. (Author's collection.)

Below: Until auto travel became the dominant mode of transportation, C.S.L.'s passenger steamers benefited handsomely from good rail connections like those pictured at Sarnia, Ontario, where the *Noronic* is alongside the pier and the excursion boat *Wauketa* of the White Star Line is departing, most likely for Detroit, her homeport. (Courtesy the Jay Bascom collection.)

Keeping Up Appearances

There was a reason C.S.L. passenger steamers were so smartly turned out: the company was very appearance-conscious.

Thus, a W. Worfolk, who was superintendent of painting for Canada Steamship, wrote in 1929, "The artistic decoration of our fleets, inside and out, has done much to advertise the C.S.L. and to make our boats second to none that sail the inland seas." He noted that "the outsides of the steamers are painted with special C.S.L. hull white … so made to stand constant washing and the vagaries of the weather" and added, "The interior decoration of our steamers is carried out in delicate tones of gray, green and ivory."[1]

Nice!

How did the company come to adopt its lovely signature all-white exterior paint scheme for its passenger ships in Eastern Canada? The minutes of a meeting of C.S.L's junior executive committee in late 1919 shed some light.

W.E. Burke, who chaired the meeting, believed that white hulls would give steamers a higher appearance in the water, improving their looks. (At the time, ships on C.S.L.'s Lake Ontario runs sported black hulls with white superstructures.) White hulls became the standard livery in 1920, and it remained in effect until C.S.L. began painting hulls of its passenger boats dark green in the early 1930s.

The company didn't neglect the looks of its ships' funnels, either. These were deemed important because, as Worfolk wrote, "The first part of a steamer that strikes the eye of the man on land is the smokestack. It has been the endeavour of our company to have the stacks on all steamers bright, clean and attractive."[2] That was true even at night, when C.S.L. stacks were illuminated by floodlight, an unusual practice for the time.

"It unquestionably has good advertising value," said a 1927 company publication of the floodlighting, "and will be more fully developed during the passenger season next year."[3]

Never let it be said that C.S.L. underestimated the value of appearances.

Workers readying the *St. Lawrence* for service in the 1947 season pose for a newspaper photographer. Also berthed nearby in this scene at Sorel, QC, where C.S.L's Montreal-Saguenay steamers wintered, are, from left, the long-idled *Rapids King*, the *Tadoussac* and the *Quebec*. (*The* [Montreal] *Gazette* photo files.)

Vessel Data

This alphabetical list of thirty ships includes only C.S.L. passenger steamers mentioned in the book. Ships are listed by the last name they had while in the C.S.L. fleet. LOA is length overall; LBP is length between perpendiculars. Length and breadth statistics are expressed in feet. Any mistakes are mine alone.

CAPE DIAMOND.

Built 1877 by J. Roach & Sons, Chester, Pa.

LOA: 265

LBP: 251

Breadth: 35

Gross tonnage: 969

Propulsion: Beam engine, paddle wheel

Ownership history: Built as *Carolina* for the Baltimore Steam Packet Co. (Old Bay Line) for service on Chesapeake Bay, acquired by Richelieu and Ontario Navigation in 1893, renamed *Murray Bay* in 1905. Passed in 1913 to C.S.L., which renamed her *Cape Diamond* in 1921. Employed on Quebec City-Saguenay run. Withdrawn from service about 1928 and sold for scrap.

CAPE ETERNITY.

Built 1910 by Detroit Shipbuilding Co., Wyandotte, Mich.

LOA: 256

LBP: 246

Breadth: 42

Gross tonnage: 1,603

Propulsion: Twin-screw propeller,

Ownership history: Built as *Rochester* for Richelieu & Ontario Navigation Co. of U.S.A., transferred in 1913 to C.S.L.'s American subsidiary, the American Interlake Line. Entered C.S.L.'s Canadian fleet in 1917 and renamed *Cape Eternity* three years later. Laid up in 1931 and sold in 1935 to a company that operated her as *Georgian* between Windsor and Georgian Bay ports. Requisitioned by the Royal Canadian Navy in 1941 for use as a floating barracks and sold to a Chinese firm after World War II.

CAPE ST. FRANCIS.

Built 1867 by William C. White, Sorel, QC.

LOA: 268.

LBP: unavailable

Breadth: 58

Gross tonnage: 2,094

Propulsion: Beam engine, paddle wheel

Ownership history: Built as *Canada* for Richelieu and Ontario Navigation Co. After sinking in a collision in 1904 was reconstructed and lengthened twenty feet, reentering service the next year as *St. Irenee.* Passed in 1913 to C.S.L., which renamed her *Cape St. Francis* seven years later. She was retired in 1921 and scrapped in 1928.

CAPE TRINITY.

Built 1911 by Collingwood Shipbuilding Co. Ltd., Collingwood, ON.

LOA: 220

LBP: 206

Breadth: 42

Gross tonnage: 2,105

Propulsion: Twin-screw propeller

Ownership history: Built as *Geronia* for Ontario and Quebec Navigation Co. of Picton, ON. Entered the C.S.L. fleet in 1913, becoming *Syracuse* the following year. Renamed *Cape Trinity* in 1920 after transfer to the Montreal-Saguenay service. Withdrawn at the end of the 1928 and scrapped nine years later.

CAYUGA.

Built 1906 by Canadian Shipbuilding Co. Ltd., Toronto

LOA: 318

LBP: 306

Breadth: 37

Gross tonnage: 2,196

Propulsion: Twin-screw propeller

Ownership history: Built for Niagara Navigation Co., which was acquired by Richelieu and Ontario Navigation Co. in 1912. Became part of the C.S.L. fleet the following year and sailed for the company through 1951. Sold to Cayuga Steamship Co. Ltd., of Toronto, which operated her 1954–1957 on the same route — Toronto to Niagara River ports — where she spent her entire career. Scrapped 1961.

CHICORA.

Built 1864 by William C. Miller & Son, Birkenhead, England

LOA: Unavailable

LBP: 221

Breadth: 26

Gross tonnage: 931

Propulsion: Paddle wheel

Ownership history: Built for the Chicora Import & Export Co. of Charleston, S.C., as a blockade runner for the Confederacy. Transferred to Canadian registry in 1866 and purchased the following year by Ontario interests, who brought *Chicora* to the Great Lakes after having her cut in two for westward passage through canals and reassembled at Buffalo, N.Y. Soon after entering passenger service she was used to transport Canadian government troops involved in suppressing the Riel Rebellion, then was chartered in 1874 for use as a yacht for Governor General Lord Dufferin before being laid up. Three years later, the Niagara Navigation Co. was formed to put her into service on the Toronto-Niagara route, where she was the spare boat by the time she entered the C.S.L. fleet in 1913. *Chicora* ran one more year for the company, between Toronto and Olcott Beach, N.Y., and was sold for use as a barge. Her career ended while in that role in 1938.

CHIPPEWA.

Built 1893 by Hamilton Bridge Works, Hamilton, ON.

LOA: 320

LPB: 308

Breadth: 96 feet at the paddle wheel

Gross tonnage: 1,514

Propulsion: Beam engine, paddle wheel

Ownership history: Built for Niagara Navigation Co. and became part of the Richelieu and Ontario Navigation fleet in 1912 after the R. and O. acquired that company. Transferred to C.S.L. the following year. After operating for forty-two seasons on the Toronto-Niagara route, she was retired at the end of the 1936 season and sold for scrap three years later.

CORONA.

Built 1896 by Bertram Engine Works Co. Ltd., Toronto

LOA: 285

LPB: 270

Breadth: 32

Gross tonnage: 1,274

Propulsion: Paddle wheel

Ownership history: Built for Niagara Navigation Co. using the engine salvaged from that company's *Cibola,* which was destroyed by fire in 1895. With the rest of the Niagara Navigation steamers, the *Corona* was acquired by Richelieu and Ontario Navigation Co. in 1912 and became part of the fleet of C.S.L. the following year, serving the company on the Toronto-Niagara and (briefly) the Toronto-Hamilton routes until her retirement after the close of the 1929 season. Sold for scrap 1937.

GERMANIC.

Built 1899 by Collingwood Dry Dock Co., Collingwood, ON.

LOA: 196

LBP: 184

Breadth: 32

Gross tonnage: 1,014

Propulsion: Single-screw propeller

Ownership history: Reportedly the last wooden passenger ship built at Collingwood, the *Germanic* began her career on the upper Great Lakes for the Great Northern Transit Co., which months later became part of the Northern Navigation Co. Destroyed by fire while in winter lay-up in 1917, four years after becoming part of the C.S.L. fleet.

HAMONIC.

Built 1909 by Collingwood Shipbuilding Co. Ltd., Collingwood, ON.

LOA: 365

LPB: 341

Breadth: 50

Gross tonnage: 5,265

Propulsion: Propeller

Ownership history: Built for the Northern Navigation Co. to carry passengers and plenty of freight across Lakes Huron and Superior, *Hamonic* served C.S.L. for thirty-two years before she was destroyed by fire at Point Edward, ON, in July 1945. Thanks to heroic efforts by her captain, all of the approximately 400 passengers and crew aboard survived.

HURONIC.

Built 1902 by Collingwood Shipbuilding Co. Ltd., Collingwood, ON.

LOA: 340

LBP: 321

Breadth: 43

Gross tonnage: 3,330

Propulsion: Propeller

Ownership history: The first of three large upper lakes steamers built for the Northern Navigation Co., the *Huronic* sailed longer than either of her two sisters, *Hamonic* and *Noronic*. She entered the C.S.L. fleet in 1913 and operated as a passenger-freight vessel until 1934, when she became freight-only; some unneeded top-deck passenger cabins were removed a decade later. *Huronic* was retired at the end of the 1949 season and scrapped the following year.

KINGSTON.

Built in 1901 by Bertram Engine Works Co. Ltd, Toronto.

LOA: 300

LBP: 288

Breadth: 43

Gross tonnage: 2,925

Propulsion: Paddle wheel

Ownership history: Built for Richelieu and Ontario Navigation Co. to run opposite the *Toronto* of 1899 on the company's Toronto-Prescott service. Both steamers came to C.S.L. in 1913, after its absorption of the R. and O. that year. *Kingston*, the longest serving paddler in the C.S.L. fleet, was retired after the close of the 1949 season and sold for scrap the next year.

LOUIS PHILIPPE.

Built in 1914 by Davie Shipbuilding and Repairing Co. Ltd., Lauzon, QC.

LOA: Unavailable

LBP: 162

Breadth: 37

Gross tonnage: 600

Propulsion: Propeller

Ownership history: Built for C.S.L. for ferry service across the St. Lawrence River between Montreal and Longueuil but ran briefly in the 1920s for the company's Northern Navigation Division between Sarnia, ON, and Port Huron, Michigan. Returned to her original route only to become redundant when the Montreal Harbour Bridge opened in 1930. C.S.L. sold her the following year to the Prescott and Ogdensburg Ferry Co., which operated her on the St. Lawrence until her retirement in 1952. *Louis Philippe* was then sold for scrap.

MONTREAL.

Launched in 1902 by Bertram Engine Works Co. Ltd., Toronto, and completed in 1905 at the Richelieu and Ontario Navigation Co.'s shipyard at Sorel, QC.

LOA: 340

LBP: 324

Breadth: 43

Gross tonnage: 4,282

Propulsion: Paddle wheel

Ownership history: The largest ship built for the Richelieu and Ontario company, *Montreal* spent her entire career on the overnight run between Montreal and Quebec. She operated on that route for C.S.L. from 1913 until 1926, when fire destroyed her while she was carrying freight after the end of the passenger season. Her hulk sank in the St. Lawrence while being towed.

NORONIC.

Built in 1913 by Western Dry Dock and Shipbuilding Co., Port Arthur, ON.

LOA: 385

LBP: 362

Breadth: 52

Gross tonnage: 6,905

Propulsion: Propeller

Ownership history: Delivered to the Northern Navigation Co. just as its fleet came under the control of C.S.L., *Noronic* spent thirty-six years sailing the upper lakes for the latter company. Destroyed by fire in September 1949 at her dock in Toronto Harbour with a loss of the lives of 118 passengers while on a post-season cruise, she was sold for scrap almost immediately afterward.

QUEBEC (I).

Built 1865 by Barclay, Curle & Co. Ltd., Glasgow, Scotland, then dismantled and reassembled by W.P. Bartley & Co. at D. & J. McCarthy shipyard, Sorel, QC.

LOA: 311

LBP: 303

Breadth: 39

Gross tonnage: 3,498

Propulsion: Beam engine, paddle wheel

Ownership history: Built for La Compagnie du Richelieu, a predecessor of Richelieu and Ontario Navigation Co. Rebuilt three times — gaining nearly thirty feet in her last makeover — she spent nearly her entire career on the Montreal-Quebec overnight service, her last fourteen years on that route for C.S.L. After her withdrawal from that run in 1927, she sailed for C.S.L. for one more season as *Ste. Anne de Beaupre*, taking pilgrims to the famous shrine of the same name just east of Quebec City. Scrapped in 1929.

QUEBEC (II).

Built 1928 by Davie Shipbuilding & Repairing Co. Ltd., Lauzon, QC.

LOA: 370

LBP: 350

Breadth: 70

Gross tonnage: 7,016

Propulsion: Twin-screw propeller

Ownership history: One of just three passenger steamers with overnight accommodations built for C.S.L. itself, rather than a predecessor company, *Quebec* was intended to hold down the Montreal-Quebec overnight service opposite her nearly identical sister ship, *Tadoussac*. Both vessels soon, however, began including the Saguenay River on their itineraries. It was while on a Montreal-Saguenay trip in August 1950 that *Quebec* was destroyed by a fire of suspicious origin. Seven passengers died.

RAPIDS KING.

Built 1907 by Canadian Shipbuilding Co. Ltd., Toronto.

LOA: 245

LBP: 230

Breadth: 41

Gross tonnage: 1,563

Propulsion: Twin-screw propeller

Ownership history: Built for Richelieu and Ontario Navigation Co. and transferred to C.S.L. in 1913. Designed for running the rapids of the St. Lawrence River between Prescott, ON, and Montreal, *Rapids King* often ran aground because she drew too much water. She underwent a downsizing in 1929 to reduce her weight (and, thus, her draft), but the onset of the Great Depression caused C.S.L. to withdraw her in the early 1930s. After lying idle at Sorel, QC, for eighteen years, she was sold for scrap in 1949.

RAPIDS PRINCE.

Built 1910 by Toronto Shipyards Ltd., Toronto.

LOA: 210

LBP: 197

Breadth: 37

Gross tonnage: 1,314

Propulsion: Twin-screw propeller

Ownership history: Built for Richelieu and Ontario Navigation Co. and transferred to C.S.L. in 1913. *Rapids Prince*, C.S.L.'s longest serving rapids steamer, was especially well suited for the Prescott-Montreal because of her shallow five-foot draft. When C.S.L. decided to retire its connecting Toronto-Prescott steamer, the *Kingston*, after the end of the 1949 season, it doomed the *Rapids Prince* as well. She never made another commercial voyage and was scrapped in 1951.

RAPIDS QUEEN.

Built 1892 by Delaware River Iron Shipbuilding Co., Chester, Pa.

LOA: 210

LBP: 194

Breadth: 34

Gross tonnage: 770

Propulsion: Twin-screw propeller

Ownership history: Registered initially in the United States as the *Columbian*, she operated for Richelieu and Ontario Navigation Co., eventually coming under Canadian registry. Usually employed on the Prescott-Montreal rapids run, she received two name changes — to *Brockville* in 1905 and to *Rapids Queen* in 1909, the year of the second of her two re-buildings. *Rapids Queen* was operated by C.S.L. from 1913 until 1929. Under subsequent owners saw service as a passenger vessel, floating hotel, barge and, finally, breakwater.

RICHELIEU.

Built 1913 by Harlan & Hollingsworth, Wilmington, Del.

LOA: 340

LBP: Unavailable

Breadth: 48

Gross tonnage: 5,528

Propulsion: Twin-screw propeller

Ownership history: Built as *Narragansett*, along with a sister ship, *Manhattan*, for a planned overnight service between New York and Providence, Rhode Island, to be operated by a division of the Central Vermont Railway. The service never materialized and after performing troop transport duties in World War I, both ships were put up for sale, with C.S.L. buying *Narragansett* and converting her into *Richelieu* at Davie Shipbuilding. As such, the deluxe cruise ship sailed on C.S.L.'s Montreal-Saguenay route from 1923 to the end of the 1965 season. Towed to Belgium for scrapping the next year.

SAGUENAY.

Built 1911 by Fairfield Shipbuilding & Engineering Co. Ltd., Glasgow, Scotland.

LOA: 290

LPB: 275

Breadth: 40

Gross tonnage: 2,777

Propulsion: Twin-screw propeller

Ownership history: Delivered to Richelieu and Ontario Navigation Co. two years before it became part of C.S.L., *Saguenay* plied the Montreal-Saguenay route for both owners. She operated in that service for C.S.L. through the 1931 season and subsequently was used only for carrying package freight. After sitting idle for many years at Sorel, QC, she was sold to Chinese interests in 1946. Wrecked in a typhoon five years later and sold for scrap.

ST. LAWRENCE.

Built 1927 by Davie Shipbuilding & Repairing Co. Ltd., Lauzon, QC.

LOA: 350

LBP: Unavailable

Breadth: 67

Gross tonnage: 6,328

Propulsion: Twin-screw propeller

Ownership history: The first and smallest of three steamers ordered by C.S.L. for its Montreal-Saguenay run, *St. Lawrence* sailed on that route until the company ended all passenger service after the close of the 1965 season. Towed to Belgium for scrapping the following year.

TADOUSAC.

Built 1879 by Harland & Hollingsworth, Wilmington, Del.

LOA: 260

LBP: 248

Breadth: 35

Gross tonnage: 1,701

Propulsion: Beam engine, paddle wheels

Ownership history: Built as *Virginia* for the Baltimore Steam Packet Co. (Old Bay Line) for service on Chesapeake Bay, she was bought in 1903 by Richelieu and Ontario Navigation Co. which renamed her *Tadousac,* oddly omitting the second "s" in the usual spelling of the word. She ran for C.S.L.'s Quebec City-Saguenay service from 1913 to 1917 and reportedly left the fleet in 1926.

TADOUSSAC.

Built 1928 by Davie Shipbuilding & Repairing Co. Ltd., Lauzon, QC.

LOA: 370

LBP: 350

Breadth: 70

Gross tonnage: 7,013

Propulsion: Twin-screw propeller

Ownership history: Nearly identical to the *Quebec* of 1928, *Tadoussac* remained on the Montreal-Saguenay route until the end of the 1965 season, after which C.S.L. eliminated all passenger service. Although slated to be scrapped, like her running mates, *Richelieu* and *St. Lawrence,* she escaped that fate, winding up at one point as a hotel and restaurant in the United Arab Emirates.

THOUSAND ISLANDER.

Built 1912 by Toledo Shipbuilding Co., Toledo, Ohio.

LOA: 173

LBP: 164

Breadth: 32

Gross tonnage: 587

Propulsion: Twin-screw propeller

Ownership history: Built for Thousand Island Steamboat Co., a U.S. subsidiary of Richelieu and Ontario Navigation Co., for service on the St. Lawrence River. In 1918, five years after joining the C.S.L. fleet, she was brought under Canadian registry and began sailing for the company out of Detroit on day excursions to nearby Ontario ports. Withdrawn in the face of growing competition from auto travel, she was sold by C.S.L. to a cruise operator in Georgian Bay but sank in November 1928 while being towed in Lake Huron.

TORONTO.

Built 1899 by Bertram Engine Works Co. Ltd., Toronto.

LOA: 281

LBP: 269

Breadth: 36 (inside paddles)

Gross tonnage: 2,779.

Propulsion: Paddle wheel

Ownership history: Built for Richelieu and Ontario Navigation Co. and inherited by C.S.L. in 1913, she spent her entire career on the overnight run between Toronto and Prescott, ON. Retired after the close of the 1937 season because of the prohibitive cost of making mandated safety improvements, *Toronto* was then laid up until sold for scrap in 1947.

TURBINIA.

Built 1904 by Hawthorne, Leslie & Co. Ltd., Hebburn-on-Tyne, England.

LOA: 261

LBP: 250

Breadth: 33

Gross tonnage: 1,064

Propulsion: Triple-screw propeller

Ownership history: The first turbine-powered ship on the Great Lakes, she was built for Turbine Steamship Co. for service between Toronto and Hamilton. Fitted with three turbine engines, she could steam as fast as thirty miles per hour. In 1906, *Turbinia* was acquired by a competitor, T. Eaton Co. Ltd., whose passenger ships became, in quick succession, members of the fleets of Niagara Navigation (1911), Richelieu and Ontario Navigation (1912), and C.S.L. (1913). After overseas service in World War I and reacquisition by C.S.L., she returned to her old route in 1924 and 1925 only to be shifted to the Montreal-Quebec day run for the next two years. Laid up in 1928 at Sorel, QC, and sold for scrap nearly a decade later.

WAUBIC.

Built 1909 by Collingwood Shipbuilding Co. Ltd., Collingwood, ON.

LOA: 142

LBP: 135

Breadth: 25

Gross tonnage: 504

Propulsion: Twin-screw propeller

Ownership history: Built for the Northern Navigation Co, *Waubic* was the last passenger ship C.S.L. operated in regular service on Georgian Bay. After eight years in the C.S.L. fleet, sold in 1921 to Rockport Navigation Co. Ltd. for service in the Thousand Islands of the St. Lawrence River. She later underwent several changes of route, name, and ownership, ending her career sailing between Nova Scotia and Prince Edward Island for Northumberland Ferries Ltd. After her withdrawal from service, she was destroyed by fire in 1959 and then scrapped.

Principal sources: Jay Bascom and Skip Gillham, *The Early Ships of Canada Steamship Lines* (Vineland, ON: Glenaden Press, 2010); Skip Gillham, *The Postwar Ships of Canada Steamship Lines* (Vineland, ON: Glenaden Press, 1998); and "Canada Steamship Lines Fleet List" at *www.marmuseum.ca*, website of the Marine Museum of the Great Lakes at Kingston. Click on "Research," then "Ship Lists," then "Canada Steamship Lines Fleet List."

Acknowledgements

What whetted my appetite for writing this book was learning that C.S.L. Group had donated thousands of historic photographs and hundreds of boxes of archival material relating to its Canada Steamship Lines subsidiary to the Marine Museum of the Great Lakes at Kingston, Ontario. In announcing the donation, the museum billed it as "one of the most significant marine history collections in Canada" and "one that provides an insight into the historical development of our country."[1]

I deeply appreciate the unfettered access the museum gave me to its veritable trove of corporate history during repeated visits to Kingston over nearly two years. Ben Holthof, then the museum's curator, could not have been more helpful in providing me with the documents and pictures I requested. And students of Canada Steamship Lines history like me can also thank Maurice Smith, the curator emeritus, who was deeply involved in securing the collection for the museum.

When it came to learning the fascinating histories of various C.S.L. passenger ships, I had the good fortune to meet Jay Bascom. I drew heavily on the meticulously researched vessel profiles — especially for the "Running the Rapids" chapter and two sidebars, "The Also-Rans" (p. 51) and "The Making (And Unmaking) of the *Montreal*,"

(p. 75) — that Jay has written as editor of *The Scanner*, the monthly bulletin of the Toronto Marine Historical Society. He also co-authored another invaluable resource, *The Early Ships of Canada Steamship Lines* (Glenaden, 2010) with Skip Gilham, author of the excellent *The Postwar Ships of Canada Steamship Lines* (Glenaden, 1998). But Jay's contribution to this book extends far beyond the aforementioned: He also permitted me to use many outstanding photographs from his collection. Not surprisingly, what began as an acquaintanceship has now become a friendship.

I also now count as a friend Benny Beattie of Montreal, who shared his memories of travelling for two decades on C.S.L.'s Montreal-Saguenay boats, first in his 1994 book, *Tadoussac: The Sands of Summer*, and then in person and through numerous email exchanges.

The task of collecting photographs besides the aforementioned ones was both pleasant and rewarding because of the invaluable and enthusiastic assistance provided by Astrid Drew at The Steamship Historical Society of America; Lynn Lafontaine at Library and Archives Canada; Marie-Paule Lamarre of the Bibliothèque et Archives nationales du Québec; Nora Hague at the McCord Museum, Montreal; Stefan Ketseti, formerly of the Sociéte Historique-

Pierre-de-Saurel, Sorel, QC; and Annie Breton and Meggie Savard of the Musée de Charlevoix, LaMalbaie, QC.

Special thanks also go to my editor, Allister Thompson, who understood my vision for *Great White Fleet* and respected my writing voice, and to his colleague Courtney Horner, who did a masterful job designing the book. My literary agent, Robert Morton, a former editor for a leading art publisher, provided wise counsel on the selection of photographs and on the book in general; he was always available as a sounding board for my ideas. And Myrna Burks, a digital artist, was a wizard at bringing out the best in well-worn pictures.

Finally, I am profoundly grateful to two individuals who have encouraged and supported me throughout this long enterprise, Myron Glucksman and my wife, Sally, to whom this book is dedicated.

Notes

INTRODUCTION

1. *World's Largest Inland Water Transportation Company, Canada Steamship Lines Limited and Its Subsidiaries,* undated C.S.L. booklet but circa 1945, 4.
2. *Ibid,* 35.

CHAPTER 1

1. Damase Potvin, *The Saguenay Trip* (Montreal: Canada Steamship Lines), undated, preface.
2. Edgar Andrew Collard, *Passage to the Sea: The Story of Canada Steamship Lines* (Toronto: Doubleday Canada Limited, 1991), 161
3. *World's Largest Inland Water Transportation Company, Canada Steamship Lines Limited and Its Subsidiaries,* undated C.S.L. booklet but *circa* 1945, 36.
4. Benny Beattie, *Tadoussac: The Sands of Summer, Memories, Stories, Legends* (Montreal: Price-Patterson Ltd., 1994), 27.
5. "The Growth of a Giant," reprint from *Canadian Shipping & Marine Engineering News,* undated but circa 1951, 21.
6. *Vol. 26* (minutes of 1943–1944 C.S.L. directors and annual shareholders meetings) April 26, 1944, annual meeting, 1355.
7. *Ibid.*
8. *Vol. 27* (minutes of 1945–1946 C.S.L. directors and annual shareholders meetings) April 25, 1945, annual meeting, 1404.
9. *Vol. 31* (minutes of 1953–1954 C.S.L. directors and annual shareholders meetings) April 21, 1953, annual meeting, 1867.
10. "CSL's Cruise Ships Retired by Board; Repairs Too Costly," *The* (Montreal) *Gazette,* Nov. 11, 1965, 37.
11. "No Longer Those Ships," *The* (Montreal) *Gazette,* Nov. 12, 1965, 8.

CHAPTER 2

1. *Niagara to the Sea,* C.S.L. brochure 1931, 4.
2. *Romantic Niagara,* C.S.L. brochure circa 1945, 6.
3. *Ibid.,* 6
4. *Niagara to the Sea,* C.S.L. brochure 1931, 32.
5. "Niagara Navigation Co.'s New Steamer," *The Railway and Marine World,* Old series, 180; New Series, 98 (April 1906), 223.
6. Jay Bascom, "Ship of the Month No.146 *Cayuga,*" *The Scanner,* Toronto Marine Historical Society Vol. XVIII, No. 8, May 1986, 6.
7. Edgar Andrew Collard, *Passage to the Sea: The Story of Canada Steamship Lines* (Toronto: Doubleday Canada Limited, 1991), 59.
8. John Maclean, "Victim of Rubber Tires, Last Passenger Ship on Lakes Retired,"

The (Toronto) *Telegram,* March 25, 1952, 17.

CHAPTER 3

1. *Wonderful Vacations on the Inland Waterways of Canada,* C.S.L brochure 1936, 3.
2. *Thousand Islands and the St. Lawrence River,* C.S.L. brochure circa 1930, 1.
3. Donald Page, "The *Huronic* and *Kingston,* A Comparison," *FreshWater,* Vol.1, No.2, Autumn 1986, Marine Museum of the Great Lakes at Kingston, 16.
4. *Vol. 16* (minutes of 1923–1924 C.S.L. directors and annual shareholders meetings) Oct. 18, 1924, directors meeting, 255.
5. *Vol. 25* (minutes of 1941–1942 C.S.L. directors and annual shareholders meetings), Sept. 24, 1941, directors meeting, 1238.
6. *Vol. 27* (minutes of 1945–1946 C.S.L. directors and annual shareholders meetings), March 13, 1946, directors meeting, 1449.
7. Jay Bascom, "Ship of the Month No. 76 Cape Eternity," *The Scanner,* Toronto Marine Historical Society, Vol. 10, No. 9, Summer 1978, 1.

CHAPTER 4

1. "C.S.L. Steamers Shoot Rapids Daily," *C.S.L. Chart,* July 1929, 4.
2. Mervyn Allan Sayer, "Passenger Steamer Shoots the Rapids," *The Australian Power Boat and Yachting Monthly Magazine,* Nov. 10, 1948, 20.
3. *Niagara to the Sea,* C.S.L. brochure, February 1926, 22.
4. "Local River Pilot Faces Risky Task," *The* (Montreal) *Gazette,* Dec. 21, 1938, 13.

5. *Niagara to the Sea,* C.S.L. brochure, 1931, 32.
6. Mervyn Allan Sayer, "Passenger Steamer Shoots the Rapids," *The Australian Power Boat and Yachting Monthly Magazine,* Nov. 10, 1948, 21.

CHAPTER 5

1. Benny Beattie, *Tadoussac: The Sands of Summer, Memories, Stories, Legends* (Montreal: Price-Patterson Ltd., 1994), 29.
2. *Niagara to the Sea,* C.S.L. brochure, February 1926, 29, 30.
3. *Niagara to the Sea,* C.S.L. brochure, 1915, 43.
4. Benny Beattie, *Tadoussac: The Sands of Summer, Memories, Stories, Legends* (Montreal: Price-Patterson Ltd., 1994) introduction.
5. *Ibid.,* 31.
6. *Niagara to the Sea,* C.S.L. brochure 1915, 49.
7. *Niagara to the Sea,* C.S.L. brochure, February 1926, 32.
8. Jay Bascom, "Ship of the Month No. 248 Montreal," *The Scanner,* Toronto Marine Historical Society, Vol. XXXI–7, April 1999, 13.
9. *Niagara to the Sea,* C.S.L. brochure, February 1926, 14.
10. *World's Largest Inland Water Transportation Company, Canada Steamship Lines Limited and Its Subsidiaries,* undated C.S.L. Booklet but *circa* 1945, 35.

CHAPTER 6

1. *Cruising America's Great Inland Seas: On the Water Highway Between East and West,* C.S.L. Northern Navigation Division brochure 1940, back cover.

2. "Time Out for Sleep," *Over the Deep,* C.S.L. Northern Navigation Division brochure 1948, section 5.

3. "Let Me See," *Over the Deep,* C.S.L. Northern Navigation Division brochure 1948, section 3.

4. *Ibid.*

5. *Vol. 26* (minutes of 1943–1944 C.S.L. directors and annual shareholders meetings), April 26, 1944, annual meeting, 1355.

6. "Under Way…Afloat, Afoot," *Over the Deep,* C.S.L. Northern Navigation brochure 1948, section 2.

7. *World's Largest Inland Water Transportation Company, Canada Steamship Lines Limited and Its Subsidiaries,* undated but circa 1945, 35.

CHAPTER 7

1. The Hon. Mr. Justice R.L. Kellock, *Report of the Court of Investigation into the Circumstances Attending the Loss of the S.S. Noronic,* (Ottawa: Government of Canada, 1949), 50.

2. *Ibid.,* 29.

3. *Ibid.,* 29.

4. *Ibid.,* 37.

5. *Ibid.,* 25.

6. *Ibid.*

7 *Vol. 29* (minutes of 1949–1950 C.S.L. directors and annual shareholders meetings), Nov. 30, 1949, directors meeting, 1622.

8. Edgar Andrew Collard, *Passage to the Sea: The Story of Canada Steamship Lines* (Toronto: Doubleday Canada Limited, 1991), 241.

9. *Ibid.,* 242.

10. "No Negligence on Crew's Par, C.S.L. Head says," *Toronto Daily Star,* Sept. 19, 1949, 13.

11. The Hon. Mr. Justice R.L. Kellock, *Report of the Court of Investigation into the Circumstances Attending the Loss of the S.S. Noronic,* (Ottawa: Government of Canada, 1949), 36.

12. *Ibid.,* 13.

13. *Ibid.,* 46.

EPILOGUE

1. Lewis Evans, *Tides of Tadoussac: The Golden Age of a St. Lawrence Resort* (Privately published in Canada, location unknown, 1982), 9.

2. *Niagara to the Sea,* C.S.L. brochure 1931, 31.

3. Lewis Evans, *Tides of Tadoussac: The Golden Age of a St. Lawrence Resort* (Privately published in Canada, location unknown, 1982), 9.

4. "Canada Steamship Lines Is Largest and Oldest Freshwater Transportation Company In World," *C.S.L. Chart,* Vol. 2, No. 7, Sept. 1. 1928, 1.

ADDENDUM: THE PEAKS AND VALLEYS OF C.S.L.'S PASSENGER BUSINESS

1. David Lancashire, "The lake vessels are not dead yet," *Globe and Mail,* May 3, 1980, 10.

2. "T.R. Enderby on Great Lakes Shipping, Coasting Laws, Etc.," *Canadian Railway and Marine World,* Vol. 33 (December 1930): 803.

3. *Vol. 24* (minutes of 1939–1940 C.S.L. directors and annual shareholders meetings), April 24, 1940, annual shareholders meeting, 1160.

4. C.S.L. *Annual Report 1941,* 7.

5. *Vol. 25* (minutes of 1941-1942 C.S.L. directors and annual shareholders meetings), April 22, 1942, annual meeting, 1262.

6. *Vol. 27* (minutes of 1945–1946 C.S.L. directors and annual shareholders meetings), April 25,1945, annual meeting, 1404.

7. "Rapids-riding Ship Service Is Eliminated: River Passenger Link Between Montreal and Toronto Discontinued," *Montreal Daily Star,* Jan. 5, 1950, 16.

8. Benny Beattie, *Tadoussac: The Sands of Summer, Memories, Stories, Legends* (Montreal: Price-Patterson Ltd., 1994), 27.

9. Benny Beattie by e-mail to the author Feb. 14, 2012.

10. "CSL's Cruise Ships Retired by Board; Repairs Too Costly," *The* (Montreal) *Gazette,* Nov. 11, 1965, 37.

11. "The Newest Thing in Holidays! Try the Auto-Steamship Vacation," *By-Water* magazine, August 1917, back cover.

12. "An Auto-Steamship Holiday," *By-Water* magazine, September 1917, 11.

13. "Just Overnight from Montreal by Palatial Steamer or Modern Highway," *Fortune* magazine ad, 1935 (month unknown).

KEEPING UP APPEARANCES

1. "Steamers Present Splendid Appearance As Paint Brushes Are Wielded at Lay-up Ports: Superintendent of Painting Tells How Job Is Done," *C.S.L. Chart,* Vol. 3, No.1, May 1929, 5.

2. *Ibid.*

3. "Jottings from the Log," *C.S.L. Chart,* Vol. 1, No. 5, Nov. 7, 1927, 4.

ACKNOWLEDGEMENTS

1. "Canada Steamship Lines Grant," *Jib Gems* newsletter of the Marine Museum of the Great Lakes at Kingston, Vol. 23, No. 1, March 2008, 2.

Bibliography

BOOKS

Ashdown, Dana. *Railway Steamships of Ontario*. Erin, ON: The Boston Mills Press, 1988.

Bascom, Jay and Skip Gillham. *The Early Ships of Canada Steamship Lines*. Vineland, ON: Glenaden Press, 2010.

Beaton, Horace L. *From the Wheelhouse: The Story of a Great Lakes Captain*. Cheltenham, ON: The Boston Mills Press, 1979.

Beattie, Benny. *Tadoussac: The Sands of Summer, Memories, Stories, Legends*. Montreal: Price-Patterson Ltd., 1994.

Burtniak, John and John N. Jackson. *Railways in the Niagara Peninsula*. Belleville, ON: Mika Publishing Co., 1978.

Collard, Edgar Andrew. *Passage to the Sea: The Story of Canada Steamship Lines*. Toronto: Doubleday Canada Ltd., 1991.

Evans, Lewis. *Tides of Tadoussac: The Golden Age of a St. Lawrence Resort*. Privately published in Canada, location unknown, 1982.

Gillham, Skip. *The Postwar Ships of Canada Steamship Lines*. Vineland, ON: Glenaden Press, 1998.

Hilton, George W. *The Night Boat*. Berkeley, CA: Howell-North Books, 1968.

Kellock, The Hon. Mr. Justice R.L. *Report of the Court of Investigation into the Circumstances Attending the Loss of the S.S. Noronic* (Ottawa: Government of Canada, 1949)

Marcil, Eileen Reid. *Tall Ships and Tankers: The History of Davie Shipbuilders*. Toronto: McClelland & Stewart, 1997.

Marine Historical Society of Detroit. *Great Lakes Ships We Remember*. Cleveland, OH: Freshwater Press, revised edition, 1986.

Minutes of the directors and annual shareholder meetings of Canada Steamship Lines, Vol. 11 through 38. Montreal: Canada Steamship Lines, 1919 to 1966. At Marine Museum of the Great Lakes at Kingston.

Young, Anna G., *Great Lakes' Saga*. Privately published in Canada, location unknown, 1965.

JOURNALS

Bleasby, J.R.G. "S.S. Cayuga and the Toronto-Queenston Steamer Service." *Fresh-Water A Journal of Great Lakes History*. The Marine Museum of the Great Lakes at Kingston, Vol. 9, No. 2 (1994), 3.

Bugbee, Gordon P. "The Saguenay Service." *Steamboat Bill*, Journal of the Steamship Historical Society of America, (Summer 1966), 56.

Kidd, Staff Sergeant James M., Canadian

Army. "Canada Steamship Lines: Kingston, Toronto & Montreal." *Steamboat Bill of Fact*, Journal of the Steamship Historical Society of America, No. 17 (August 1945), 314.

Page, Donald. "Canada Steamship Lines: The Fleet Develops, 1913 to the 1980s, A Shipbuilder's Perspective." *Freshwater: A Journal of Great Lakes Marine History.* The Marine Museum of the Great Lakes at Kingston, Vol. 3, No. 2 (Winter 1988), 5.

Page, Donald. "The Huronic and the Kingston, A Comparison," *Freshwater: A Journal of Great Lakes Marine History.* The Marine Museum of the Great Lakes at Kingston, Vol. 1, No. 2 (Autumn 1986), 15.

"Pictures in Review," *Freshwater: A Journal of Great Lakes Marine History.* The Marine Museum of the Great Lakes at Kingston, Vol. 9, No. 4 (1994), 19.

"Ship of the Month," a regular feature of *The Scanner,* journal of the Toronto Marine Historical Society. TMHS has profiled *Cape Eternity, Cape Trinity, Cayuga, Chicora, Chippewa, Hamonic, Kingston, Montreal, Rapids Prince, Rapids Queen, Saguenay, Toronto,* and *Turbinia,* among other ships. The "Ship of the Month" index and profiles published in out-of-print issues are at *www. tmhs.ca.*

MAGAZINES AND NEWSPAPERS

"C.S.L.'s Cruise Ships Retired by Board; Repairs Too Costly," *The* (Montreal) *Gazette,* Nov. 11, 1965, 37.

David Lancashire, "The lake vessels are not dead yet," *Globe and Mail,* May 3, 1980, 10.

John MacLean, "Victim of Rubber Tires, Last Passenger Ship on Lakes Retired," *The* (Toronto) *Telegram,* March 25, 1952.

"Local River Pilot Faces Risky Task," *The* (Montreal) *Gazette,* Dec. 21, 1938.

"Mervyn Allan Sayer, "Passenger Steamer Shoots the Rapids," *The Australian Power Boat and Yachting Monthly Magazine,* Nov. 10, 1948, 21.

"Niagara Navigation Co.'s New Steamer." *The Railway and Marine World,* Old Series, 180; New Series, 98 (April 1906), 223.

"No Longer Those Ships." *The* (Montreal) *Gazette,* Nov. 12, 1965, 8.

"No Negligence on Crew's Part, C.S.L. Head Says." *Toronto Daily Star,* Sept. 19, 1949, 13.

"Rapids-riding Ship Service Is Eliminated: River Passenger Link Between Montreal and Toronto Discontinued." *Montreal Daily Star,* Jan. 5, 1950, 16.

"The Growth of a Giant." Reprint from *Canadian Shipping & Marine Engineering News,* undated but circa 1951, 21.

"T.R. Enderby on Great Lakes Shipping, Coasting Laws, Etc." *Canadian Railway and Marine World,* Vol. 33 (December 1930), 803.

CANADA STEAMSHIP LINES PUBLICATIONS

"An Auto-Steamship Holiday." *By-Water* magazine, Vol. 2, No. 7, September 1917, 11.

Annual reports for most years between 1931 and 1968.*

"Canada Steamship Lines is Largest and Oldest Freshwater Transportation Company in World." *C.S.L. Chart,* Vol. 2, No. 7, Sept. 1, 1928, 1.

Cruising America's Great Inland Seas: On the Water Highway between East and West. Northern Navigation Division brochure, 1940.

"C.S.L. Steamers Shoot Rapids Daily." *C.S.L. Chart,* Vol. 3, No. 3, July 1929, 4.*

"Jottings from the Log." *C.S.L. Chart,* Vol. 1, No. 5, Nov. 7, 1927, 4.*

Niagara to the Sea brochures for 1915, 1926, 1930, 1931, 1935, 1938, and 1939.

Over the Deep, Northern Navigation brochure, 1948.

Potvin, Damase. *The Saguenay Trip.* Undated booklet, preface.

Romantic Niagara, brochure circa 1945, 6.

"Steamers Present Splendid Appearance as Paint Brushes Are Wielded at Lay-up Ports: Superintendent of Painting Tells How Job Is Done." *C.S.L. Chart,* Vol. 3, No. 1, May 1929, 5.

"The Newest Thing in Holidays! Try the Auto-Steamship Vacation." *By-Water* magazine, Vol. 2, No. 6, August 1917, back cover.*

Thousand Islands and the St. Lawrence River. Brochure circa 1930, 1.

Wonderful Vacations on the Inland Waterways of Canada. Brochure 1936.

World's Largest Inland Water Transportation Company, Canada Steamship Lines Limited and Its Subsidiaries. Undated booklet but circa 1945.

*Publication at Marine Museum of the Great Lakes at Kingston.

Index

Numbers in italics refer to images and their captions.

The early
Canadian trade routes
of the canoe, bateau &
sailing ship ••• plied
now by freight and
passenger vessels of

*Canada
Steamship
Lines*

Passenger Lines ———
Freight Lines ———

① Duluth — Terminal
② Fort William — Terminal & Grain Elevators
③ Port Arthur — Terminal & Transfer Point
for Western Canada & Pacific Coast

④ Sault Ste Marie Warehouse & Coal Do[ck]
⑤ Sarnia Terminal & Coal Dock
⑥ Midland — Grain Elevator & Coal Doc[k]
⑦ Queenston Terminal

Raymond DaBoll '44